The Goat Ropin @ Raccoon Run

Goat Roping- Something totally uncontrollable.
A confusing disorganized situation attributed to
human error. A convoluted issue contested by
many parties. Chaotic and unorganized. Totally
and disastrously wrong. Nothing to be done but
sit back and watch the train wreck.

This work is a fictionalized version of many
events and rounds of golf played by the author
and his companions over a 62 year period.
Enjoy this story.
I enjoyed telling it.
CjP

The Goat Ropin' @ Raccoon Run

* * *

by
Chip Prezioso

The Goat Ropin @ Raccoon Run
Copyright © 2021
Chip Prezioso

Comments:
cprezpawleysisland@gmail.com

ISBN:
Paper Back   978-1-950768-30-1
Hard Cover   978-1-950768-31-8

Prose Press
Pawleys Island, SC
prosencons@live.com

Foreword

The GOAT ROPIN @ RACCOON RUN is highly fictionalized. It is based on an amalgamation of characters I've crossed paths with over my 67 years. If you see yourself in one or more of these characters, go get some psychiatric help. Most of the events really happened…. just not over a two day period between Columbia and St. Matthews. Alcohol consumption is exaggerated, a little.

Reading the glossary first would be very helpful to the non-golfer or anyone who hasn't been brought up south of the Mason Dixon line. **(PAGE 116)**

Voka and Buttweiser (vodka and budweiser) can confuse you and are used throughout the story.

I owe my wife, Roxanna a debt I could never repay and I'm not just talking about this book. My son Chase has seen a small portion of these escapades growing up around this group. Like Jumbo, he can hold his own in a "goat ropin".

Again, the names have been changed to protect the guilty and this recounting of this adventure is not meant to hurt any feelings or embarrass anyone. If you think you may be a part of this group, you've got no feelings left anyway. CjP

Chapter I

The sleek goldenrod Rolls Royce Corniche glided up to the drive-through window at Hardee's. It was 7:30 a.m. on a warm August Saturday morning. Marvin, wearing his chauffeur's cap, threw his arm across the honey beige glove leather seatback and announced our arrival.

"You gentlemens wanted biscuits for the ride to St. Matthews?" he announced.

Beaver, having been dragged half-clothed from his penthouse apartment 15 minutes earlier, immediately perked up at that information.

"You know I love me some sausage biscuits," moaned "the Beav." "Marvin, get me four. Anyone else want one?"

"You deserve a Mexican Breakfast after being late like that," barked Chic. "Make it two steak for me."

"Me too!" said Davo. "What's a Mexican Breakfast?"

"A cigarette and a good piss," cracked Chic. "Make that four steak biscuits, Marvin. Du, how about it? Want to change your luck with a biscuit this morning?"

Du laughed. "My luck is fine; you know I brought my breakfast," which consisted, as it did every morning, of a bag of dry roasted peanuts, a can of Coca Cola, a Zero candy bar, and a copy of The State newspaper. "Thank you very much!"

Chic passed a twenty to Marvin and said, "Get what you want, Marvin."

"Oh, no sir, I couldn't risk getting nuttin' on these fine Coruthian leather seats! Mr. Dryer would kill me!"

Marvin was perhaps the most trusted employ-ee at owner Dick Dryer's car dealership, and his only choice for this task: transporting four golfers of questionable maturity and sanity some 120 miles to a small-town member-guest tournament, passengers in Dryer's $200,000 Rolls Royce automobile.

"Go ahead and get something, Marvin, one of us will drive while you eat," offered Chic.

"Oh, no sir, Mr. Dryer tolds me absolutely no one but me was to drive this fine automobile."

Weeks before, during an afternoon of Cape Cod Coolers in a crowded 19th hole, Beaver had maneu-vered Dryer into granting him the use of a Rolls Royce for the Saint Matthew's Member Guest. The next day, after some sober thought, Dryer had limited the use to one day and "generously" provided a chauffeur, Marvin, resplendent in a chauffeur's cap. Still, it was a windfall for the crew.

Chapter II

This wasn't the group's first golf outing, or "goat roping". The four had literally been raised together. Within two years of each other in age, Chic, Du, and Davo lived in the same neighborhood, had attended the same schools, church, Little League, and learned to play golf at the same country club. They could finish each others' sentences and read each others' minds. Hell, brothers were rarely this close.

Their "routines" and pranks had been perfected over 20-plus years. Innocent bystanders were victims of their hi-jinks, and all but the most sophisticated or streetwise fell into their traps. Beav was several years younger than the others and had been raised to play his role. He knew things no teenager should have known at his age. They all delighted at providing a "set-up" or delivering the "coup de gras".

Du was blessed with extraordinary hand-eye coordination, but his body struggled to keep up. A picky eater, he was rail-thin and had always had some sort of physical ailment. His high IQ and keen powers of observation made him an aggravating smart-ass, especially when coupled with this group. He chose to sit out his second semester of his freshman year at the University of South Carolina. During that time, his body matured, and he became an extraordinary golfer. His classic swing flowed like molasses in winter, and he was simple in his approach and execution.

Du decided to return to Carolina when Chic entered as a freshman. Roommates in the athletic dorm, they continued their journey together on a golf team the university showed little interest in. Chic and Du rigged the election and became Co-Captains and player-coaches for all intents and purposes. The University would periodically appoint some "retiring" football coach to chaperon the team to tournaments. Each spring the team would show up in Florida for the first event of the season. Dick Copas and Jesse Haddock, legendary coaches of Georgia and Wake Forest, would ask Chic and Du, "Who's your coach this semester, guys"?

Chic and Du made formal introductions for the first couple of events but when the chaperon changed so often, they couldn't keep the names straight, they'd point at the "out of place looking guy" who looked like a football coach. Team discipline, training rules, and practice schedules weren't an issue as they were self-coached.

During the gas shortage of the early seventies, the team resorted to hitting practice shots down the two football fields behind the athletic dorm's dining hall that were primarily used by the track team. This didn't please the track coach and he constantly complained that his guys were stepping on their golf balls and getting "stone bruises". Chic and Du knew the team's players were using their own practice balls and picking them up; they needled that they were helping their track buddies with their agility if they occasionally had to sidestep an errant ball. Needless to say, this comment didn't go over well when repeated to the track Coach, Bill McClure, he went up in a "puff" (of smoke) and they were officially banned: barred from using their only practice facility within reach, with no gas and no place to practice within 20 miles.

The two co-captains huddled, and with some consultation with key team members came up with a solution: "Happy Hour" The team's activities consisted of classes from 8 a.m. until 1 p.m.; lunch; a trip to a Putt-Putt course; then 4 p.m. Happy Hour at the Twilight Lounge. At 6 p.m., they were back at the dorm for dinner, followed by a shower and change of clothes.

At 7:30pm, Chic and Du would return to the athletics dorm's dining hall to watch the football team "feed," a sight they likened to dropping by the Coliseum in Rome to watch Christians being fed to the lions. The football team consumed massive quantities of food; whole slabs of beef being shoveled into their gaping "pie holes." It was eating on a scale no normal person could imagine.

Brother Davo being a football team captain, Du

and Chic were granted special access to this spectacle, while cautious to hold any "needling" of the big jocks to a minimum. This was largely an act of self-defense, since many football players were jealous that the golfers' scholarships were the same as theirs but seemed to require much less work. Throw in the fact they would be leaving the dining hall to "monitor" the football players 'girlfriends' activities at the local college bar scene – one the football team was forbidden to enjoy during its season – Chic and Du wisely treaded lightly

CHAPTER III

One particular evening, Du was running a bit late and Chic was at the table with brother Davo and Steve Courson, who would later star for the Pittsburgh Steelers' offensive line – and later famously blew the whistle on steroids use in the NFL. Chic was engaged in what little polite conversation could be had with mouths full when he heard a voice behind him calling his name. He turned to see who was summoning him but saw no one he knew. The second time he heard "Chic!" he looked up to see Jim Carlen, the newly hired head football coach and the school's athletics director, motioning him to join him at his table.

Chic doubted this was going to be a social visit. He anticipated an "ass whipping!" The anticipation of an ass whipping is often worse than the ass whipping. Carlen was very polite, asking him to take a seat next to him. "You're the captain of the golf team, aren't you?" the coach asked. His "radar" pinging away, Chic replied, "Actually, I'm a co-captain," figuring Du should get a full share of whatever was coming.

"Well good," Carlen said. "Maybe you can help me with a problem I'm having?"

"Sure Coach, anything we can do to help," Chic quickly replied.

"Do you think you guys could keep the women out of your rooms, and stop all of the cocktail parties?" Carlen said, a wry grin on his face. "Coach Richardson's son lives in that dorm and is about to have a heart attack. He's regaling his dad with stories of Sodom and Gomorrah style golf team parties."

Coach Bobby Richardson, who had played second base for the New York Yankees during their heyday, was always active in the Fellowship of Christian Athletes and had stepped up his involvement after his retirement from the majors. Having had notorious drinker Mickey Mantle as a teammate, he was no stranger to aberrant behavior. Having it in the same dorm with his team, however, was a different matter.

Chic, thinking fast, decided to opt for honesty – sort of – over a "what women? What parties?" approach with Carlen. "Ah, sure, coach, I'll take care of that immediately if not sooner," he said, a semblance of an earnest expression on his face.

Carlen eyed the other coaches, as if to say, "See, that's how it's done." After enjoying his display of authority, the coach looked at Chic and said, "Now, is there anything I can do for you?"

Having just had a "get out of jail free card" dropped in his lap, Chic couldn't believe he was now being offered a "make a wish" to boot. Knowing Carlen was an avid golfer, he slowly started his pitch.

"As a matter of fact, there is something you could do that would help us quite a bit," he told Carlen. "What's that, son?" the coach replied, bequeathing a fatherly smile on Chic.

"Well, coach, the gas shortage has made it impossible for us to get to the nearest golf course to practice," Chic said. "We drive our own cars, but 40 miles round trip is a stretch with gas rationing in place."

"What can I do?" a now-interested Carlen asked.

"We'd like to hit our practice balls down the two unused football fields behind the dining hall," Chic said.

"Well why can't you do that?" Carlen asked.

Chic pointed toward the track coach, who sat unsuspectingly across the dining hall. "Coach McClure says we leave our golf balls on the field, and his guys step on the balls and get stone bruises," he said, adding just a bit of sarcasm to his answer. "Coach, the golf balls are ours and we pick them up," he added. "If his track guys aren't smart or agile enough to avoid a couple of golf balls, they deserve stone bruises." And Chic gave the coach his winningest smile.

"Well, son, let me see what I can do about that," Carlen said, leaning back in his chair. Chic, knowing that once you get a positive answer, you don't stick around and muck it up, stood and said, "Thank you very much, coach, and it was nice to meet you gentlemen," nodding to the other coaches.

As Chic strode towards the dining hall exit, he heard Carlen behind him saying, "Don't forget about that other matter we discussed." With his personal "Eddie Haskell" perched on his shoulder, Chic turned and said, "Yes sir, coach, I'm heading downstairs to handle that right now." A big grin came across Carlen's face, and Chic knew he had his deal.

It probably didn't hurt Chic's entreaty that his brother, Davo, was a co-captain of the football team and lived on the first floor of the athletic dorm. Undersized for a starter at 6 feet, 225 pounds, Davo was formidable from his constant time in the weight room. A legendary "badass," he loved the contact football allowed. The press loved the fact he was a local boy and had even earned a scholarship by walking on and trying out, and that his dad was the last three-sport letterman at the university.

Most men cut him a wide berth, including an unfortunate soul who had threatened him with a gun one evening outside a college hangout. Davo told the gun-wielding gunslinger, in front of several bystanders, "If you miss, I'm going to feed you that gun." That was enough to send the hoodlum running down the street.

Then there was Beaver, the youngest of the four, who tagged along behind his older brothers, learning things no teenager should have known. Beav was a wise ass whose charm and blond good looks could be turned on and off at the blink of an eye. He was molded to play his part in the cast from an early age.

Each brother knew the entire routine and took pride in their ability to play any part even in a quickly evolving situation. Beav enjoyed the ladies, and one evening after escorting a college girl back to her dorm – Beav was a high school junior at the time – he called Chic after midnight.

"Chic, I've totaled Mom's car!" he squawked. "Come get me, please, and hurry!" He quickly issued directions and Chic started across town to retrieve the Beav. As everyone knows, every accident in your Mom's car is a total, and Chic chalked that part up to exaggeration. It wasn't until Chic was about to turn off the interstate and two Highway Patrol cars zoomed by him at 85 miles per hour that Chic began to worry.

Knowing the area better than the patrolmen, Chic arrived at the accident site ahead of them. There in his headlights, he saw the Beav, clothes shredded, bleeding from the head and chin, and barefoot. "It takes a hell of a lick to knock your shoes off," Chic thought to himself. While examining the Beav, Chic looked over his bloody shoulder and saw their mother's baby blue Ford Crown Victoria, upside down on the railroad tracks, at the bottom of a ravine, on fire.

Soon, the patrolmen arrived and started questioning the Beav. Chic politely mentioned the name of their commanding officer, and suggested they could question Beav at the Richland Hospital where he was taking his brother. They agreed, and one patrolman stayed behind to work the accident while the other tailed them. At the hospital, the officer followed Beav and the physician into the back.

Several minutes later, the doctor returned with a permission slip, allowing them to pull a syringe of the Beav's blood for a test. Chic asked what procedure they intended to perform on his brother that would require a blood test; the doctor said all they could find wrong with him was about four cuts that would require 100 stitches to close, including his foot and chin, which would be very painful. Asking why they'd need a blood test for that, Chic was told Beav's alcohol level could react with the painkillers and cause heart attack or stroke.

Guessing that a blood test would probably reveal a DUI's worth of alcohol in the Beav's system, Chic thought for a moment. "Stitch him up without painkillers," he told the doctor. The irate patrolman stormed out shortly after that, having made sure Beav started the procedure with no painkillers. All the Beav had to do now was explain to their mother how her new Crown Victoria had been barbecued beyond recognition. Compared to that ordeal, the stitching would be nothing.

Chapter IV

And so it began, South Carolina golf's version of "Animal House comes to Green Acres": four skilled, experienced raconteurs invading a community steeped in tradition and rules passed down through generations of planters. Raccoon Run and St. Matthews were blissfully unaware of the storm headed their way in a "yeller Rolls."

Liquid refreshments had been meticulously procured, prepared, and packed. About the time the Rolls made a sweeping turn onto Highway 601, the biscuits had been consumed and were being washed down with "Transfusions," a delightful concoction of Welch's Grape juice, ginger ale, and voka (southern for Vodka). As "Free Bird" cranked up on the Rolls' stereo system, someone fired up a "doobie." Without credit or blame, the lit joint made its way around the Rolls' interior.

Marvin was apoplectic, although he didn't know that word. He did know what Mr. Dryer would do if that Rolls came back reeking of marijuana or had a cigarette burn in that fine honey-beige "Coruthian" leather!

"You gentlemens please throw that cigarette out!" Marvin pleaded. "Here, I'll roll down the windows for you gentlemens," as he fingered the automatic window controls.

The crisis was averted. The cigarette didn't last long. At 70 miles an hour, with four windows rolled down, the smoke billowed harmlessly from the cabin. It was still 20 minutes to Raccoon Run.

Chapter V

One year earlier, Chic and his dad were cruising down the same stretch of Highway 601 in his Buick Park Avenue, heading toward the inaugural Calhoun County Country Club Member Guest. Dad's childhood friend Paulie was his partner for the event. Chic had been recruited to play as Paulie's friend Junior's partner. As they started across the Gorge, Chic asked, "What's the course like?"

Dad thought for a moment before he replied. "I played it once a couple of years ago," he said. "The front nine is cut out of a soybean field and the back nine runs along a creek bottom. Push-up greens and no irrigation back then. Depending on the amount of rain they've had and crop prices, it could be an airport runway or a tropical rain forest.

"But", he added, "the farmers are very proud of it and try to compete with Orangeburg County Club, 15 miles down the road. These guys are successful farmers but there is a lot of difference between growing crops and growing and manicuring a golf course. You and I and Richard Humper will be 'celebrities,' having been in the newspaper and TV for playing and winning state-wide competitions. That's a big deal to these folks."

"Slippery Dick (Richard Humper's nickname) will be here?" Chic said, surprised he'd be playing in an obscure event like this.

"Yeah, he sells Junior's father life insurance," Dad explained. "He's the largest farmer in the county so it's pretty much a command performance."

"Any good local players?" I asked.

"Joe Fairey is playing with his dad, the local Cadillac dealer, according to Paulie," Dad said.

"I know Joe. He's my only Clemson friend," Chic said, laughing.

The big four-hole Buick bounced into the dirt parking lot, its dust cloud partially obscuring an old sign reading "St. Matthews Country Club: Members Only." Everyone called it "Raccoon Run" or in local slang, "Coon Hall." Paulie and Junior were waiting in their customized golf carts as we pulled into a level spot.

The customized carts were a status symbol, to be sure, and the members took full advantage of this quirk in the club's bylaws. Customization ranged from over-sized electronic coolers to Rolls Royce grills, to custom paint jobs, bucket seats and stereo systems. Paulie's cart was regaled with University of South Carolina, "Game-cock Garnet and Black" paint, matching seats, and a garnet button that, when pushed, played a crowing rooster. Not to be outdone, Junior's buggy sported custom Clemson purple paint trimmed in blaze orange.

Junior, although not a Clemson graduate, bled purple, not orange, like most Clemson fans. Purple cart, purple seats, shorts, socks, and shirt, all purple. The purple cap that covered his orange hair was emblazoned with an orange Tiger paw. Junior sat up many evenings drawing "circles" and 'JR' on his new Titleist golf balls in purple magic marker, years before it became an accepted practice on the PGA Tour. This exercise was very time consuming, as Chic later came to find out that he needed around 11 balls to complete a round.

Paulie and Junior pulled up and began loading Chuck and Chic's golf bags on the appropriate cart while they changed their shoes. Junior sprang from his cart, thrust out a muscular, heavily freckled hand and said, "Hey Punkin, I'm Junior, your partner!"

Chic took half a step back and glanced over his left shoulder, trying to figure out who "Punkin" was. Caught off guard, he left his hand there for an awkward couple of seconds before recovering. Shaking his hand, Chic said, "Damn glad to meet you Junior, let's get 'em!" Hopping into the cart with his Dad and Paulie behind them, off they went.

Chapter VI

Few athletic endeavors are as physically exhausting and mentally draining as five hours of hunting golf balls through acres of snake-infested swamps and sun-baked bean fields in the Lowcountry of South Carolina. Chic's game was awful, but his partner thought he was Arnold Palmer. As Junior peppered him with questions from the first tee, Chic made the mistake of correcting Junior's alignment, resulting in a "good shot!" from the erstwhile "instructor." From there on, every shot he hit had to have Chic's approval. As Junior's head filled with swing thoughts, his body seized up like a failing pump motor.

After an hour or so of constant chatter, hunting purple striped golf balls and killing snakes, their playing partners took to some serious beer drinking in self-defense. Between the constant search for errant shots, urinations, and requests for more coldbeer, the round seemed as if it would never end. Mercifully, it did, and Chic headed straight to the bar for a drink of liquor and to wait for his Dad to finish.

Sitting at the Bar behind the eighteenth green, Chic could tell from Dad's posture he was as ready as Chic was to "skedaddle" back to Columbia. As he and Paulie finished, Chic met him coming off the final green and handed him a freshly poured gin and tonic. Normally not much of a drinker, his big mitt reached out and snatched the drink from Chic's outstretched hand. Adjusting the cup to keep the lime from interfering, he chug-a-lugged half the drink, in one swallow. As the half empty cup cleared from in front of his dark brown eyes, Chic could see the look of desperation fade to relief.

Paulie tapped in his handicap-aided birdie putt and loudly announced, "I hear that makes us leaders in the Clubhouse!" Chuck in return shot him an embarrassed grimace. As they headed to the scoreboard, just left of the outside bar between the eighteenth and the clubhouse, Paulie and Junior commenced lobbying Chuck about spending the night and having dinner with a group at Junior's "plantation."

Chuck politely declined and quickly headed into the men's locker room to freshen up for the trip home. Paulie and Junior spotted Chic at the bar collecting "toters" for the "ditch," also known as drinks for the road. Starting in on Chic, they pleaded, "Can't you talk him into staying?"

"Uncle Paulie, you know my mother?" Chic asked with a raised eyebrow. Paulie dropped his head as he nodded yes. Coming out of the locker room at almost a trot, Chuck accepted the refill, slowing to politely speak to several of the participants. He then headed toward the parking lot and the sanctuary of his Park Avenue with Chic, Junior, and Paulie in tow.

Catching his eye, Chic stretched his arms out, imitating a wide receiver. He loved to drive his Dad's car and Chuck gracefully flipped him the keys, leading him by a foot as a good quarterback would. Climbing into the car, Chuck was still receiving details from Paulie about Sunday's festivities.

"Bring Lou!" Paulie shouted as the door of the running car closed. Fat chance, Chic thought as he turned the air conditioning up to max. Glancing into the rearview mirror, he wheeled the quickly accelerating Buick onto the road. A cloud of dust enveloped Junior and Paulie. To anyone watching from the clubhouse veranda, their departure resembled a jailbreak.

After a couple of minutes of silence on the road while they cooled off, sipping their cold beverages, and relaxing in the luxurious cabin, Chic broke the silence. "Well, how'd you play?" he asked

Dad slowly turned toward him and shook his head. "Chic, I've never been so embarrassed in my life!" he moaned. "Paulie threw the ball, he kicked it from behind trees, and had five 'carries' on the back side – for sixty yards! Hell, he even kicked my ball 20 yards up the fairway out of the rough. Cheating on a scale I've never imagined!"

"Twenty yards is a pretty impressive kick," snickered Chic.

"What did you do?" Chic asked, knowing his Dad would not have condoned that behavior.

"I told him to stop and he ignored me," Dad said. "I just stayed as far away from him as I could after that. If I go back tomorrow, it will be my last trip." Winking, he added, "My back feels like it's beginning to stiffen up."

"Wow!" Chic exclaimed.

"How was your day?" Dad asked.

"The only two balls Junior hit solidly all day came when he stepped on a rake at the fifth green!" Chic joked.

Dad chuckled. "That bad?"

If it had been a fight, the referee would have called it, Chic told him. "If I'd had some left-handed clubs, I'd have had him try hitting it from the other side," Chic said. "His swing couldn't have been worse. After two hours of hunting golf balls with purple markings and killing snakes, a 'drunk front' rolled in: our playing partners were trying to dull the pain with 'Dr. Buttweiser (southern for Budweiser).

"They were either pissing or hunting more coldbeer the whole round," Chic said. "If there were any rule in the book disallowing you to piss every other hole, they'd have been DQ'ed (disqualified) on the front nine." He groaned. "My back is feeling a little stiff, too."

"You're only 29," Dad replied. "You can't use that excuse. Find your own."

"Your football knee should be your malady; I'll take the back, okay?" Chic said.

Dad laughed and settled back into his plush seat for the ride home.

Sunday was uneventful, pretty much a repeat of Saturday's round. Chuck's poor play, which he attributed to an old football knee injury, was highly unusual but assured that he and Paulie had no chance of finishing in the money. Junior assured Chic he would be working on his game and made him promise, in a weak moment, to play as his guest the next year.

Begging off the tournament finale, a fish fry at Junior's lake house, Dad and Chic headed back on U.S. 601 to Columbia, reliving the characters and events they had been witnesses to that day. Little did they know there would a "sequel" a year later.

Chapter VII

Marvin turned the Rolls into the dirt parking lot, but Chic quickly directed him to a particular spot. "No, Marvin, park over there to the right near the putting green," he said.

"But sir, the sign says, 'Reserved Club President,'" Marvin said, sounding worried.

"I got this, Marvin," Chic replied. "He's a friend of mine. He told me I could use it; he's not playing." That seemed to calm things.

Marvin quickly adjusted his turn and swept the huge yellow Corniche into the paved spot in front of the clubhouse, dust cloud following. The foursome was fashionably late, sixteen minutes ahead of the shotgun start, and outside the clubhouse, all eyes were glued to the parking lot. News of their participation – aided by Paulie and Junior – had spread like wildfire.

Davo, a former captain of the South Carolina Gamecocks football team and a legendary "bad ass," would replace Chuck as Paulie's partner this time. Du, a

two-time state amateur champion who had missed qual-
ifying for the Masters by one match a year ago, was to be
the partner of Rose, Paulie's wife.

A real stunner, Rose wasn't much of a player, but
no one cared. Her outfits and her "waggle" made up
for any weaknesses in her golf game. Just watching her
tee the ball up was a religious experience – or as Junior
described it, "Enough to make a dog break a chain."

Beaver was teamed with Doc, the town barber who
wore a dentist's tunic while cutting hair and playing golf,
earning him his nickname; come to think of it, no one
had ever seen him wearing anything else. Junior was of
course waiting for Chic.

From the front seat, after adjusting his chauffeur's
cap, Marvin said, as a crowd gathered, "You gentlemens
give this dust a minute to settle and I'll come open the
doors." Marvin, aware of his audience, was precise in his
movements.

Walking in front of the car, he opened Chic's door.
Adjusting his shades, Chic slowly exited, waving to a
couple of folks he knew in the crowd. Junior appeared
from the settling dust in a new, all-purple golf cart. He
was resplendent in his new matching purple hat, shirt,
shorts, socks, shoes, and golf tees. Soybeans must have
fetched a good price this year. His orange hair and freck-
les set off against his outfit.

"Wow!" Chic exclaimed. Junior grinned with pride
as he choked back the dust.

Everyone busied themselves preparing for the start, some twelve minutes away. Bags were moved from the Rolls' trunk onto customized golf carts and coolers were offloaded. Everyone was shaking hands, exchanging pleasantries, and getting a hug from Rose.

As Chic changed shoes at the trunk, he spied Beaver still in his t-shirt and gym shoes. "Beav! Time to suit up!" he hollered, tapping his left wrist, and frowning at him. Beaver being 6-foot-3 and 240 pounds, it was a friendly reminder.

Beav opened the door and hopped into the empty back seat of the Rolls. Tinted windows up, Beaver "drew" the shades and locked the doors. Seeing this, Marvin frantically felt his pockets for the keys. A relieved look came over his face as he felt them. He was still terrified that any damage would befall the Rolls on his watch.

Just then Paulie came up behind Chic and said, "Hey, I want you to meet our new Head Pro, Jeff ... "

"Adams," Chic said, finishing his introduction.

Jeff had been the assistant pro at Orangeburg Country Club, where Du and Chic had won the South Carolina Team Championship the year before. Jeff stood 5-foot-3 in cowboy boots, which he always wore. A jealous little man with a sugar-bowl haircut and a Napoleon complex, he was itching to exercise his authority.

"Hello, Chic. Quite a group you assembled here?" he said.

"All friends of Paulie's," Chic replied.

Jeff reached out his hand and as Chic shook it, he stretched his left arm up to Chic's shoulder – a stretch for him – and said with a tone of menace in his voice, "This is Mr. Deals' parking space."

"I know; Billy called me and asked me to use it as he was going to be out of town this weekend," Chic replied evenly. "He must have forgotten to tell you." And he turned back to the group.

Expecting a reply, Chic looked up just in time to see the large yellow door of the Rolls swing open. Out popped the Beav, all 6-foot-3 and 240 pounds of him: clad in bright red shorts and a triple extra-large multicolor golf shirt adorned with a bright yellow lightning bolt, florescent blue stripes and bright red stars that matched his shorts. White golf shoes and a white Kangol driving cap completed his outfit.

Arms lifted in clenched fists, he thrust his hips forward a couple of times, shouting, "Anybody want to get you some of this?" Obviously, he had been working on his "entrance" for a while. Caught off guard, everyone stood dumbfounded with their mouths hanging open.

Davo broke the silence. "Jesus Christ, Beaver, you look like a giant screen TV that's just been hit by lightning!" That broke up the crowd that by now had swelled to about 30. Beav knew he'd been skewered and dropped his shaking head as the "belly laughing" continued.

Recovering quickly, Beav threw a big arm around a

startled Marvin and said, "Come on, Marvin, let's get us a drink before the round!" The new arrivals joined them as they strode toward the clubhouse, for one "last" drink before the round.

Jeff Adams had not been laughing and quickly realized what was about to happen. The whites-only "sanctity" of Coon Hall was about to be violated. No one could remember a black person other than an employee being inside the clubhouse, much less using the front entrance or sitting down for a drink.

Jeff bounded up the second step – an effort for him in the cowboy boots – just ahead of the assembled mob, with Beav leading the way, Marvin held in a friendly headlock/bear hug. Hardly noticing Jeff appearing in front of him, Beav gently swept him aside.

Jeff stammered, "You can't ..." as the crowd following Beav pinned him against the railing. Paulie, Junior and Chic helped Jeff from his sitting position as the crowd passed. Paulie attempted to calm a rattled Jeff, suggesting at this point the remedy might be worse than the offense. Besides, he needed to tidy himself up before making his announcement in front of the assembled participants in 10 minutes.

Thankfully, the shotgun starter had already been dispatched to his appointed spot in the middle of the hallowed grounds of Coon Hall... A good thing, as Jeff may have been tempted to fire the starting gun somewhere other than into the air.

Chapter VIII.

The forty customized golf carts, neatly lined up on the manicured lawn behind the clubhouse, resembled the allied armada heading for Omaha Beach. Above them, Jeff sauntered up to the veranda railing to start his announcements. Nervously, he accidentally keyed the microphone of the bullhorn; the loud "squelch" scared everyone including Jeff but did have the effect of getting everyone's attention. Even the crowd gathered around Rose's cart for a "good luck" hug started towards their carts.

Du, headed back to his cart from the locker room, surveyed the neatly arrayed golf carts before him. A slight grin came across his face as a plan formed in his devious mind. Oh yes, this was perfect, closely packed, everyone wandering, no one paying attention.

He hadn't counted, but a quick survey told him a new world record was within reach, right here at Coon Hall. Too late to try for today, but tomorrow with a minor diversion, immortality would be his.

Jeff nervously made it through scoring, local rules,

Mulligans, gimmes, and the barbecue commencing shortly after the round. Stumbling through most of it, he finally keyed his walkie-talkie, and a shotgun blast rang out across the hallowed grounds of St. Matthews Country Club. The assembled battalion of golf carts started out. Electric carts starting faster than the sputtering gas versions. Heading quickly to their assigned holes, each driver had his own idea of the fastest route. Collisions were narrowly avoided as cross words were exchanged. With a little devious help, Du thought the start had all the makings of a "goat rodeo!"

Beaver and the Doc were playing with Du and Rose. Davo and Paulie, paired with Junior and Chic, followed out to start one hole behind them.

Chapter IX

Chic's foursome had drawn the seventh hole, a par-3 not far from the clubhouse. They played their shots into the green while others were still positioning themselves. Rose's skimpy designer outfit enhanced her model's figure, which Junior always described through glassy eyes as "enough to make a dog break a chain!" Her group was slowed by each passing group stopping to "wish Rose luck" and ogle her one last time.

As Chic's group putted out on the seventh green, Beav, Doc, Rose and Du were preparing to hit their tee balls off the par-4 eighth hole. Angling slightly through a soybean field, the ladies' tee was 30 yards ahead of the men's tee. As Rose sashayed up to her tee, every eye was on her. As she slowly bent over to tee up her ball, the four of them almost fainted.

Paulie thrust out his chest in admiration, proud as a peacock of his wife's display of womanhood. She waggled her entire body a couple of times and unleashed a magnificent drive, splitting the fairway. Unable to further contain their admiration, Du and the Beav sprinted the 30 yards to the ladies' tee, whooping and hollering the entire way.

Beaver reached Rose first and wrapped his huge arms around her, lifting her off her feet as he gave her a big bear hug. Suddenly, mid-lift, there was a "pop." Beaver later described it as sounding like the guide wire on a light pole popping, followed by an "unraveling" twang. Rose's eyes got big as Beaver lowered her to the ground. She knew instantly what had happened and quickly tried to cover her ample, free-roaming breasts. Her bra, already stretched to its design limits, had given way under Beav's bear hug.

Her club already on the ground, she placed a hand on each shoulder, her elbows strategically crossed at her chest. Immediately everyone knew what had happened, though no one knew how to react. Rose, by no means a bashful woman, said as her reddened face slowly broke into a smile, "I need to get these pups under control!"

Everyone howled. Rose, screened by Paulie, deftly reached inside her blouse and removed the malfunctioning garment. Emerging from behind her grinning husband, she held up the lacy bra for all to see. She now had a legitimate excuse to continue as she could have preferred originally – a huge distraction, to be sure.

Chapter X

The round continued with few other distractions. Beaver at one point warned Du, a notoriously picky eater with a sensitive stomach, "Wait 'til you get a taste of this Lowcountry barbecue! You'll be able to crap in a Pepsi bottle, it's so spicy! I hope you put a roll of toilet paper in the freezer this morning. You'll need it!"

As the round progressed, with the effects of the heat and alcohol taking over, even the "free roaming pups" novelty waned. They were still observed and admired, but worship gave way to competition. Du decided things needed livening up.

The seventeenth hole ran through a swamp to an elevated green, a par-3 of 147 yards. After an 8-iron shot to about 14 feet, Du slid behind Doc and the Beav's cart, his spikes "clicking" on the asphalt; the hole was one of few with a paved cart path that ran from the tee across a dam up to the green. With a nonchalant flip of his wrist, the clasp on the strap holding Doc's golf bag in place opened, and the deed was done.

Beav and the Doc both reached the green with their tee shots, a cause for celebration. Du was already in his cart, taking Rose to the ladies tee some 25 yards forward. Doc high-fived the Beav as he flipped his 6-iron into his bag. Beav shoved his 9-iron into his bag and slipped behind the wheel, right leg fully extended, jamming the accelerator to the floor. The cart jumped, slamming Doc against the seatback, as simultaneously Doc's unclasped golf bag flipped backwards off the cart, grinding, and scrapping the hot asphalt.

Beaver, some 10 yards down the path, slammed on the brake while dropping his shaking head. He too had fallen victim on many occasions to Du's signature prank. He did not even need to look.

Doc was out of the cart screaming, "My new clubs! My new bag!" As he ran to inspect the damage, Beav passed him at full speed in reverse. Doc hollered "Watch Out!" as Beav jammed on the brakes, hitting the reinforced bottom of the bag with the cart's bumper, pushing it another five feet.

Doc commenced screaming again, inconsolable at the thought of his new fancy equipment being prematurely battle-scarred. Doc's life philosophy was always, "It's much better to look good than to be good."

Rose's mouth, cherry-red lipstick glistening in the sun, hung open as she tried to comprehend the cause of this sudden mayhem. Du on the other hand was casually sitting with his left leg over the seat rail, left arm over the seatback, sipping his "Big Orange," which consisted of equal parts voka and club soda. A large orange slice accompanied the concoction but could be omitted in emergencies.

Admiring his handiwork, Du mused loudly, "Probably needs to check the fastener."

Chapter XI

After refreshing themselves and reloading coolers at the main bar behind the eighteenth green, the group continued at the first hole, their twelfth hole of the round. Du and the Beav had found Marvin resting in a shady corner of the veranda and persuaded him to ride along with them, "fireman style," on the back of the carts.

Marvin chuckled. "I'm glad you gentlemens rescued me; those folks kept ordering drinks from me," he said. "I tried to explain I wasn't working there. They were not happy when I told them that."

"Well, come on Buddy, you're with us now, Du said.

Doc seemed a bit woozy playing the first hole. He may have over-served himself after consuming a double "Transfusion" at the clubhouse: five ounces of voka, 10 ounces of Welch's Grape Juice, all the ice you could pack into a 32-ounce double stadium cup, adding Schweppes Ginger Ale until it overflowed.

Doc could hardly believe five ounces of voka in this

hot sun could finish him. As he wobbled up to his putt for par/net birdie at the first green, "Doctor" Beav decided he needed a shot of adrenaline. Pulling the flag from the cup, Beav stepped a couple of feet directly behind his partner and said, "Left edge now, Doc, knock it in."

As Doc drew his putter back to stroke the ball, Beav whipped the flag inches over his head. The whizzing of the pole and flutter of the flag zipping by his head caused Doc's knees to buckle and he lost control of his bladder.

He fell to the ground as the ball fell into the cup. This wasn't the Beav's first "rodeo" and he had timed the swing perfectly, allowing the putter to impact the ball before the "sonic boom" of the passing flag hit Doc. Rolling around in his wet britches, he pleaded, "Holy Jesus! Holy Jesus! Help me, Holy Jesus!"

Rose rushed to help him, but as she knelt over him, the "pup with the brown nose" peeked out of her blouse. Struggling to help the prone Doc, she pushed the unruly pup back into hiding. About then, she caught a whiff of the Doc's escaped bodily fluid.

Du quickly stepped in and grasped her elbow, preventing another victim from hitting the turf. Davo, Junior and our group 100 yards down the fairway were belly-laughing so hard, it was difficult to stay on our feet.

Our group played through the second hole as Du and the Beav attempted to revive Doc and Rose. Beav appeared remorseful as he applied ice-cold towels and straight grape juice to Doc, although he was still snickering a bit. Du was attending to Rose as Paulie came to her side.

Satisfied there was no lasting damage, Paulie shook his head at the Beav, more in admiration than admonishment. Cool towels and grape juice brought Rose around quickly. Fortunately, in that heat Doc's britches dried quickly and there was no lingering odor.

Rose, again unsure of what had triggered *this* episode of mayhem, busied herself with returning to her pre-stumble composure. This wasn't like any kind of golf she had played with the girls. This was more like a drunken brawl that stopped occasionally to hit a golf shot.

As our group, now playing ahead, hit our second shots, the fairway cleared for Du, Beav, Doc, Rose, and Marvin. Doc, still not steady on his feet, rocked a bit as he teed up his ball, finally resorting to squatting to stick the tee in the ground. Then gingerly placing the ball onto the tee.

Du whispered to the Beav, "I believe I can finish him off before we're done." Beaver, normally not the compassionate type, eyed Du and said, "Don't you think he's had enough?"

Du replied, "You know what Chic says: Never give a sucker an even break. Besides, he's a Clempzon fan!"

"Good point," replied the Beav.

They hit their shots and hopped into the carts, Marvin tagging along, fireman style – he seemed to be getting the hang of this game. Both groups played the next several holes without incident, other than Junior killing a large rattlesnake while searching for an errant shot.

Marvin didn't like that at all: not Junior killing the snake but becoming aware that he was that close to large reptiles. He became "clingy" after that, not straying far from the golf carts or the "cut grass." At one point, he was even coaching "Mr. Junior," telling him, "Cut his head off and he'll grow another one!"

On the fifth tee, with three holes left to play, Marvin didn't like how close Du's cart had gotten to the undergrowth. At the last minute, he decided to climb onto Beav's buggy as Beav hit the gas. Marvin, off balance, falling back and arms grasping, managed to grab the tallest club on the cart: Doc's new $300 graphite metal driver.

No match for Marvin's 175 pounds, the loud "pop" of the graphite shaft snapping alerted everyone to Marvin's fall. By the time the carts had stopped, and everyone was turning around, Marvin was getting to his feet with what appeared to be an 18-inch Tiger-headed popsicle: Doc's club's head-cover on a frayed, splintered graphite stick. The stunned silence was pierced by Doc screeching as he realized what had happened.

"That's my brand new $300 graphite metal driver!" he screamed. Beav restrained him with a big bear hug/head lock. Escorting him over to Marvin, Beaver took the "Tiger Puppet," raising it into the air and saying to no one in particular, "It wasn't like you were hitting it all that well anyway?"

The incident instantly erased any steps towards sanity that Doc had made over the past several holes. Whether it was the alcohol, heat, or reversals he had suffered that day, Doc buried his face into Beav's massive shoulder and cried like a baby. Taking a sip of his ever present "Big Orange," Du blurted out, "Careful, Beav; he might piss himself again!"

Rose took Doc from Beav's grasp and, while keeping a safe splatter-proof distance, soothed the spent Doc. Watching from the fairway, we were enjoying this hilarity, not needing to hear the dialogue to know what was going on. This was funnier than Tim Conway's dentist skit with Harvey Korman on the "Carol Burnett Show" – our benchmark for comedy.

With Marvin apologizing to Doc, order was eventually restored, and the round staggered towards a welcome conclusion.

Chapter XII

All four players hit their tee shots safely onto the green at their final hole. Finishing at the sixth hole, we drove ahead to watch them putt out on the seventh. Du pulled the flagstick out of the hole, carefully handing it to Marvin while eying Beav with a smirk on his face. Everyone positioned themselves to watch Rose as she finished.

She didn't disappoint, one-handing the ball from the hole and throwing in a leg kick for good measure. A tailored skort flashed her shapely thighs, instead of the ladylike stoop she'd been using all day. With no teams behind us, we gathered to exchange scorecards and check totals.

Although the clubhouse was only a short ride away, refreshers were mixed and sipped as Paulie went over the post-round festivities and schedule. The barbecue would be served and continue into the early evening. Famously renowned Lowcountry pulled pork with many varieties of sauces would be available. Scores would be tallied, teams divided into flights and re-paired, putting an end to the shenanigans witnessed that day.

If, as Davo was prone to say, "Ridicule is the sincerest form of flattery," Doc had been flattered half to death. Golf etiquette would prevent us from "flattering" a stranger like that tomorrow.

Marvin checked his watch: 4:45 pm. Mr. Dryer had given him strict instructions that "the Rolls had better be back at the dealership sparkling and locked up by 7 p.m." Marvin whispered this update to the Beaver.

In a rare moment of clarity, Beav announced to the group, "Okay guys, we've got to get going, just time to freshen up, grab a quick bite of that barbecue and hit the road." Paulie, Rose, and Junior wailed, "You can't go! You've got to stay for the party!"

Beav elected not to disclose the fact that he had a date at 8 p.m., a sweet young thing he'd just met. The Beav's recuperative powers were legendary but after today, tonight would be a challenge even for him.

"Nope, we'd love to stay but I promised Mr. Dryer I'd have Marvin and the Rolls back by 7 p.m." he said. "Besides, we're all in contention and the 'too-nee-ment' starts tomorrow." With appeal sounding futile, everyone jumped into the buggies for the short drive back to the clubhouse.

Beaver had wedged the remnant of Doc's driver between the roof and frame at the front of their cart, a Tiger banner of sorts. Buoyed by this clever use of his once-prized graphite metal driver and Tiger head cover, the Doc looked forward to the envious comments from all the other Clempzon fans.

As the other three carts started away, Beaver slowly climbed into their cart. Looking over at the Doc, he said, "You ready?" Doc smiled at the Beav and raised his cup in a symbolic toast and said, "Hit it!"

Beav push the pedal to the floor, the cart lurched forward, flipping Doc's unclasped golf bag on to the other paved path at Coon Hall. Neither Doc nor Beav turned to see what had happened. Both knew.

Looking ahead, they saw Du, left leg over the seat rail, left arm over the seat back, slowly taking a sip from his "Big Orange." Looking over at Rose, he said, "Probably ought to have that clasp checked."

Rose chuckled, finally getting it. Marvin hopped from the cart and hurried down the path to reload Doc's battle-scarred bag and clubs onto the cart. He made sure the clasp was functioning and doubled the strap through the clasp.

Tapping the cart twice with his ring hand he, he said, "That ought to get you to the clubhouse, Mr. Beaver," as he hurried back to Du's waiting buggy. Doc, his head in his hands, slowly turned to the Beav, straightened himself and pointed toward the clubhouse as a smile gradually appeared on his face.

Realizing his trial by fire was nearly at an end, Doc began to perk up, his mood almost jovial. He had taken more ridicule than anyone would have thought possible. Instead of whining about his $300 splintered graphite driver, when a passerby commented on his cart's "Tiger banner," he said, "I wasn't hitting it all that well. It looks better where it is," and winked at the Beaver.

Even Du gave him a "thumbs up" on overhearing that quip. Doc dismounted and strode confidently toward the locker room.

Chapter XIII

Jeff Adams, scowling, approached the carts. "Got your cards ready to turn in?" he asked. "We've got to flight and pair everyone; got a 10 o'clock shotgun start tomorrow morning. You guys aren't going to be running this tournament again tomorrow!"

Handing the diminutive pro both cards, Chic said, "Oooh-kay, hotshot, chill out! We've been helping you out, telling all of the members how you've been insisting Marvin relax in the clubhouse."

Jeff's eyes, now being big as saucers, stammered, "I didn't know . . ." as Chic turned and called over his shoulder, "Come on guys, let's get some barbecue and clean up for the ride home. Marvin will get the bags loaded and the car cooled off. Marvin, we'll bring you a sandwich."

A small crowd was gathering around the big yellow Rolls Royce, still parked in Billy Deal's space. Marvin had it cooling in the late afternoon sun as he meticulously polished some of the smudged chrome. Although the president's space was paved, a thin coat of dust had settled over the Corniche from parking lot traffic. Marvin had his work cut out for him as he nervously patrolled the area, trying to keep the curious away from the car.

One hour and 25 minutes until 7 p.m., and realizing Marvin's deadline for departure was quickly approaching, Chic shouted across the crowded veranda, "Beav, don't you have a date in a couple of hours?" Stopping in mid-sentence, Beaver spun on his heel and headed towards the Rolls, gathering Davo and Du do along the way.

Quickly saying their goodbyes, the group hurried through the packed veranda with Beaver leading the way to the waiting ride. Marvin had the door open as they approached, urging them on.

"You gentlemans got to hurry! We ain't got no time left," he shouted, closing the door behind them. After shaking a few hands and kissing a few babies, the group climbed into the luxuriously cool cabin. After shutting the door, Marvin wasted no time hopping into the driver's seat. The car seemed to start moving back as he hit the seat and the group waved to the assembled crowd of well-wishers like they were rock stars.

Just as the Rolls started forward, a golf cart pulled in front of the car, blocking their path. Marvin groaned, "We got no time for this!"

Paulie, Rose and an immaculately dressed golfer stepped out of the cart. As the back window rolled down,

Rose stepped up, her fresh beautiful face beaming. She laughed and said, "I've never had so much fun on a golf course! I'll never forget today's round. Be careful, and we'll see you tomorrow."

As she stepped away, Paulie stepped up to the window and said, "Wish you guys were staying but I think we all need some rest after that round." With quick farewells, he stepped away and the "fashion plate" stuck his head in the car window. Immediately, the group recognized his voice: "You're the wildest bunch of sumbitches I ever met," he said.

Their mouths fell open; it was the Doc! He had trashed the grape juice- and grass-stained dental tunic, the urine-stained shorts and had purchased an outfit right off Jeff's pro shop mannequin. The shower didn't hurt, either. His finger looped over the lip of a blaze orange solo cup, as he sipped his own "Big Orange."

"See you tomorrow!" He toasted the crew as Marvin rolled up the window and headed towards 601. All heads were turning, watching in disbelief as Doc put his arm around Rose to escort her to the clubhouse.

Chapter XIV

Chic piped up as they rode away. "Paulie's not going to be happy with that move. He will whip the Doc like a rented mule if he sees him groping Rose!" he said.

"We may have created a monster," Beav chimed in. "They say clothes make the man!"

"Did the guy that sold you that shirt tell you that?" Du asked Beav with a grin. "They probably gave you a bowl of soup with that shirt, right?"

Marvin opened up the big Rolls and it crossed the Congaree River Bridge hitting 90 on the three-quarter mile straightaway. Davo handed a C-note up to Marvin about halfway across, saying, "Thanks, Marvin, you were great!"

The $100 bill fluttered onto the glove leather seat as Marvin paid full attention to the road ahead, making up some time. From the back seat Du said, "What time are you picking us up tomorrow, Marvin?"

Marvin was wide-eyed by now, trying to pilot the rocketing Corniche down the narrow two-lane bridge while eying the $100 bill on the seat, just out of reach. Caught off guard by Du's question, he stammered, "Mr. Dryer didn't say nuttin' 'bout Sunday."

Beav cleared his throat and mumbled, "We only had the car for today." Dryer, a wise man in certain respects, had weighed his options and calculated the odds of the Rolls making it, unscathed, through two days with this crew at less than 50 percent.

Davo, coming to Beav's defense jumped in. "You know Jumbo's got that Suburban. He'd love to come with us," he said. Thinking the proposal over for a moment, Chic laughed. "I think there is a three 'Prez' limit in Calhoun County," he said, "and Du counts as a Prez, so that puts us at five. Probably a big fine!"

Du piped in. "Great idea," he said. "It would be worth paying a fine to see Jumbo put on an eating exhibition at the barbecue and fish fry."

Jumbo was Chic, Davo and Beav's younger brother, 19 years old and tipping the scales at 285 pounds. At 6-foot-3, he was a pretty good knife and fork man.

"Davo, how about call Jumbo and get him to meet us at the Beav's, say at 7:30 tomorrow morning," Chic said. "Call him early and bribe him with the barbeque and fish fry. He's probably working tonight. If he goes out after they close, we'll be driving ourselves."

The conversation turned to events of the day. "Hey, you guys did a heck of a job on the Doc today," Chic said. "Turned him from a 'cheese dick' into a player;

honestly, I thought he was a goner, laying there on the first green after pissing himself!"

Davo agreed. "Yep, that was the turning point. He could have gone either way there: either sucking his thumb in the cart for the rest of the round or dusted himself off."

"You mean drying himself off?" Beav said. The correction drew snickers from everyone. "From what we saw when leaving today, I'd say we made a man out of him today," Chic said.

From behind the wheel, Marvin, who had been listening intently, added, "I sho' feels bad about breaking the Doctor's golf club."

Stirring from a trancelike state, Du spoke up. "I've got two or three extras at the house; I'll try to bring him one tomorrow," he said. "Beav, I'd leave that broken driver up on the golf cart; the Doc seemed to play better with it up there."

"So, Beav, who's the victim tonight?" Du asked, referring to Beav's date. "Cute little blonde that works at the highway department," Beaver said.

"Not a client again, I hope," Chic said.

"Nope, I know better than that," Beaver replied.

"Oh yeah, I remember that public safety chick that you pissed off," Chic said. "We haven't sniffed a nickel's worth of business since that episode."

An aggrieved Beaver responded: "I had no idea she was married! Du, you've been married a long time; you ever get any on the side?"

Du pulled down his Ray Ban Aviators, adjusted himself in the big leather seat and, with a surprised look on his face, responded, "Damn, I didn't even know they had moved it!"

That response broke up the cabin, while Marvin swerved trying to control the Big Rolls and howling out loud.

It had been a good day, all right, almost home and no casualties. The car, in need of a good cleaning, was otherwise unscathed. As they approached Beav's building, the scene of legendary shenanigans, Chic reviewed assignments and Sunday's schedule.

"A 7:30 a.m. departure," he said. "Davo, you'll have Jumbo here, his Suburban emptied, gassed and ready to roll."

"Aye, aye, Captain," Davo replied and saluted.

"Everyone okay to drive home, Davo, Du?" asked Chic. There were nods from both as they claimed their belongings from the trunk, thanking Marvin as they did. Chic kissed his left hand and patted the roof of the Rolls. Turning to shake Marvin's hand with his right hand, Chic slipped him a fifty-dollar bill.

"Thank you, Marvin, a real pleasurable day."

Beaming, Marvin hugged Chic and, with a tear in his eye, shook his head, climbed into the Rolls and was gone.

Chapter XV

Sunday dawned bright and clear. Unbelievably, everyone was present and accounted for. Promptly at 7:34 a.m., the big silver Chevy Suburban pulled into Beaver's parking lot next to his work truck, a Ford Explorer. Chic noticed the Beav's grey Jaguar XJ 12 parked in the garage with its cover in place.

"Hey Beav, I thought you had a date last night?" Chic asked.

"Yeah, turns out I had double-booked myself, so I canceled both," Beav said. "I had a case of the voka virus. As soon as I hit the couch, I was out cold. The phone woke me at 8:30 p.m. Both called later to check on me. I surely would have been caught. They are both chomping at the bit, trying to get a shot at the title!"

Beav was known widely as Columbia's most eligible bachelor. The Number One catch in Columbia: tall, blond, good looking, with a great line of bullshit. The penthouse condo and Jaguar didn't hurt that reputation. He knew women and loved them, and they loved him back. Each evening, the elderly women living in his building would gather in a sitting area near the door he used, hoping to get a glimpse of him coming or going. He always had time for them and a kind word, complimenting their hair or outfits. They often baked for him and would try to set him up with their granddaughters.

Beav enjoyed the baking but wisely shied away from the setups. To keep his ego at a manageable level, we would embellish stories about his laziness. Like, look up the definition of "Gypsy Rich" in the dictionary and you'll find Beaver's picture. Or Chic's favorite line: "Beaver hates to work on Wednesdays because it ruins both weekends."

Jumbo and Davo hopped out of the big Suburban, hollering, "Let's go, if you're waiting on us, you're backing up!" Davo, proud of his logistical coup, was directing the loading. Large as the Suburban was, it took every usable inch to hold five grown men, four sets of golf clubs, six coolers, shoes, and a change of clothes for everyone.

"You mean to tell me you got all of this into a Rolls Royce yesterday?" asked Jumbo.

"We may have an extra cooler or two and a change of clothes we didn't have yesterday, but the Rolls was a behemoth," Chic said, with all nodding in agreement.

"We've also got this little package Freddie brought me last night. We didn't have it yesterday," Beav said, gently holding up a rucksack sack he'd placed in the seat next to him.

"What's that?" asked Du.

"You remember us telling you about a friend bringing us the artillery simulator he lifted from National Guard duty?" Beav said.

"Oh yeah, equal to a half stick of dynamite," Du said. "You guys threw one off of Beaver's balcony at midnight one Saturday, right?"

"Yep, from the 18th floor," Beav said, laughing. "The city lit up like a Christmas tree. You should have heard the police monitor, people reporting air raids, terrorist bombings, real Wrath of God stuff."

"We should have been ashamed of ourselves," Davo added.

"You've got another one of those?" Chic said, blinking. "What do you plan to do with it?"

Beav thought a second. "I'm not sure," he said, "but I thought it might come in handy."

"Oh my," Chic stammered, shaking his head.

"Besides, another one of those things going off around here could send me to the pokey," Beaver said. "It wasn't too hard for the cops to figure out where that last one came from."

As the Suburban pulled out of the parking lot, Chic chimed in, "No, Jumbo, turn left, we've got to run by Hardee's for biscuits!"

"Nope," Davo said, proudly holding up four large Hardee's bags. "Jumbo and I already took care of that."

Chic's mouth hung open as he muttered, "You're

kidding, amazing!"

With Du having his usual breakfast of roasted pea-nuts, a Coke and a Zero candy bar while scanning The State newspaper, there were three biscuits apiece. Jumbo would clean up the extras while moaning, "You know I love sausage biscuits!"

Jumbo wheeled the big SUV to the right and off they went. Sunday, August 24, 1980: a date that would live in infamy.

Chapter XVI

The drive to St. Matthews was uneventful, mostly consisting of conversations and lore surrounding the Beav's prolific love life. Always informative, sometimes educational, and often fascinating, the topics were wide ranging. Finishing the Zero candy bar, Du asked, "You still using that 'red patent leather spike heel shoe in the backseat' routine?"

"What?"

"You've never heard about that routine, Jums?" Beav said. "It came to me in a dream. You know how competitive women are with each other?" Everyone nodded.

"Well, when I meet a new one, I whine and tell them how I haven't had a date in months," Beav continued. "I drop my head to show them how vulnerable I am. Works like a charm. On the appointed evening, I'll show up at their front door, slicked up, Jag detailed. As I open the door for them, they spot in the empty silver leather backseat of the XJ12, one spiked heel, red patent-leather open-toed shoe. Game on, she knows she's

got a player on her hands and the competition has be-
gun."

Everyone was snickering and hanging on "the Master's" every word. After a dove shooting trip to Argentina, Beaver's prowess with the local *senoritas* earned him
the title "Maestro di Chicas." Loosely translated "Master of the Girls," the women were of Spanish and Ital-
ian descent, so Beav's blond good looks had them eating
out of his hand. We shortened the name to "Maestro,"
which Beav adored.

"Really, you'd be surprised how important the placement of the shoe is to the whole scheme," he said. "It can't
look placed or staged. Much harder than you think."

"It would have to be," Chic said in a needling tone.

Ignoring the comment, "The Maestro" continued
his lecture. "I just pull one from the velvet bag I keep in
my gun safe," he said.

Chic interrupted again. "Right or left?" he asked.

"Right or left, what?" Beav replied.

"Shoe, dummy," Chic snapped.

"You could have been asking which side of the back
seat," Beav retorted.

"Oh, I figured that out: right behind her seat so
she'd see it getting into the car," Chic said.

"And to a rookie like you, that should make sense,
but women are curious, like cats," Beaver said. "Once
seated, while I'm walking around the front of the car, they
always turn to their left to inspect the small backseat."

Everyone was shaking their heads in agreement, basking in the genius of the "Maestro," who then added, "I experimented a lot with placement before settling on my technique."

"I can't wait to hear this," Chic said.

"Yep, very scientific; I stand outside the passenger side of the Jag, open that long door, push the seat forward, and with my thumb and forefinger, I pinch the tip of the heel and flip the shoe onto the backseat behind the driver's seat."

"Play it as it lies?" asked Chic, invoking a golf rule.

"Normally yes, but to be honest I have taken a 'mulligan' if the position is just not right," Beav said.

"But no placing," Chic said.

"Nope!" Beaver emphatically replied.

"Just one more question," said a now fully invested Chic. "Right or left?"

"I knew you'd ask that. Left! Always, unless I don't get lucky on the first date, which seldom happens; then I'll switch it up and go right, to change my luck."

"And if you do get lucky?" Chic asked.

"The shoe goes back into the velvet bag and into the safe."

"Do they ever ask about the shoe?" Chic asked.

"Never. Not one so far," Beav said.

Chic could not contain his admiration. "Remarkable!" he said.

Chapter XVII

"Listen up, after the round, Junior wants to show us around his farm," Chic said as they continued toward St. Matthews. "The fish fry is at his lake house, so let's get to the Suburban as soon as we can. There'll be someplace to shower and change before the party. It should be fun. Beav, we've got to talk about that 'firecracker' you've got and what you plan to do with it."

"You don't trust me?" Beaver said, looking hurt.

"In a word, NO!" Chic replied. "In two words, HELL NO! I'm just saying: it's dynamite. Someone could get hurt, like me. I'm no doctor but I'll bet that label says don't handle under the influence of alcohol. Du, you're being mighty quiet."

Sounding thoughtful, Du replied, "Do you realize there will be at least 40 golf carts lined up ready for the shotgun start? My record is 15. I could shatter that, a new world record. If I can manage a small diversion, I think it's possible."

"I'll help," Davo said.

"Count me in," the Beav chimed in.

"Me too," Jumbo said.

"Oh brother!" Chic rubbed his head. "Check your wallets. Let's see how much cash we've got between us."

"What's the money for?" Davo asked.

"Bail!" Chic said emphatically. "Malicious mischief and mayhem would be likely charges if no one dies." Chic reeled off the possibilities, anticipating chaos while wondering how yesterday's shenanigans hadn't resulted in death or dismemberment.

Chic continued his talk as Jumbo wheeled the Suburban into the Presidents' parking spot. "Okay boys, Rule Number One, no lampooning the locals," he said. "We're guests. And remember safety first."

Everyone was laughing as they piled out of the SUV. Standing there waiting was Jeff Adams, arms crossed, all 5-foot-3 of him, in his trademark cowboy boots. Snarling at the inattentive group, he said loudly, "You guys aren't taking over this tournament again today."

At 6-foot-3, Du towered over the diminutive pro, he flicked his sunglasses to the bridge of his nose and said, "Ooo-kay, hotshot. Chill." With 30 minutes before the start, Du threw an arm around Jeff as his diversion, fully formed, took shape in his already alcohol-dulled brain.

"Had you thought about an invocation before the start?" Du said. "That might be just the ticket to calm some of these high-jinks. It is Sunday, you know."

Jeff was thrilled that someone of Du's celebrity would take an interest in him. Beaming, he looked up at

Du and said, "You know, I could … "

Shaking him off, Du continued. "Great idea, Jeff. Rose, introduced by you out on the veranda, would be perfect." Like that, Du had his diversion.

Chapter XVIII

Jumbo helped lug coolers and clubs to the formation of 40 golf carts neatly arranged below the veranda across the back lawn. As Jumbo loaded Du's bag onto his cart, Du prowled the expanse of staged carts, unfastening clasps that held the bags to the carts as he went, this required a great deal of stealth and skill. He could barely contain his glee as he considered the "masterwork" about to be unveiled. He worked the milling crowd like a campaigning politician, opening clasps as he went down the rows of players making last-minute preparations. He would get as many as he could now and recheck during the announcements.

Rose's instructions would include her asking everyone to stand up front during the Lord's Prayer, giving Du an open field for one final inspection. After all, how many times would he get the chance to set the new World's Record for "bagging," the name Du had given his malevolent art.

Jumbo finally caught up with Du as he was completing his initial walk-through.

"Du, where you been?" Jumbo asked.

"Oh, just shaking a few hands and kissing a few babies," Du said. "What's up?"

"I found an extra driver in your bag while I was loading it on the cart and I knew you wouldn't carry two. I wanted to know which one I should put back in the truck."

"Damn, I'm glad you reminded me, Jums," Du said. "I've been so busy ..." He caught himself, saying, "that other one is for the Doc. Marvin snapped the head off his driver yesterday falling off the cart."

"What?" Jumbo asked.

"Rookie mistake, never mind, I'll tell you later," Du said. "I've got to find the Doc."

Just then Du spied Paulie, Rose and a guy that looked like the actor George Clooney walking towards them. Du flicked his shades down to make sure his eyes hadn't deceived him.

"I'll be damned," blinked Du.

Stepping around Jumbo, Du grabbed the driver, pivoted, and gave Rose a big bear hug. This time, her bra held. Du smiled and whispered, "Just checking. Hey gorgeous, I need a favor."

"Anything," Rose said, winking.

"Good morning, Paulie, how they hanging?" Du said to Rose's husband. Before Paulie could answer, Du stepped over to the Doc and handed him the driver, looked him in the eye and said, "It's much easier to look good than to play good, but this may help your game."

Patting him on the back, he said, "You've got the look part covered."

"Thanks Du," grinned the Doc, waggling the driver. He was indeed a new man after Saturday's transformation that would've broken lesser men.

"Partner, I need a quick word, please," as Du beckoned to Rose.

After a short conversation, Rose nodded her understanding and set off in search of Jeff. Du then turned his attention back to the Doc.

"Doc, you may want to swing that stick a couple of times before the gun goes off," he said. "The shaft is probably stiffer than your other club and the loft is probably a little lower. Try teeing it higher and taking a longer swing. With those new duds and that big stick, you should be on fire today."

Fired up by Du's pep talk, Doc hurried off to hit a few practice shots. Shouting back over his shoulder while grinning like a mule eating briars, the stylishly attired Doc said, "Thanks, Du."

Fifteen minutes before the shotgun start, everyone was involved in their personal warm-up routines: stretching, swinging weighted clubs, hitting a few practice shots, checking equipment, and mixing a "toter." Junior showed up in a brand-new purple outfit head to toe. Under his arm, he carried a dozen freshly purple-marked Titleists. Paulie was working the crowd on his way to Rose's cart where Du was relaxing and sipping a freshly concocted "Big Orange," with orange slice. A crowd was gathering, and Paulie sensed an opportunity to retake control of the event. After all, this was his club, and these were his guests.

"You guys really did a number on Doc yesterday," he announced. "I've never seen a baptism of fire like that and I've been around! He may be a little overconfident now; he's all over Rose. I may have to open up a Number Two can of 'whup ass' on him if he gets any more confident with my wife."

Davo stepped in. "Paulie, he's just trying out his new sea legs."

"I'm going to jam one of those sea legs up his fancy ass if he doesn't back off!" barked Paulie as his face and neck reddened.

"You know we are heading right over to Junior's as soon as we finish the round," Paulie said. "He's dying to show you guys around his farm. Wait until you see the place. Make sure he takes you into the Old Barn. In 1965, his dad received some sort of crop subsidy and went to Columbia and bought a brand-new Lincoln Continental. It's sitting right there in the barn where he parked it when he drove it home from the dealership. It's got 64 miles on the odometer, mint condition. I got them a cover for it 15 years ago."

"Wow, we've got to see that" squealed the Beav.

"Maybe I can take it for a spin," he added, a gleam in his eye.

"No chance, no way, forget it, Beav," Chic scolded.

Before Beav could protest, the megaphone squealed. "Five minutes to get to your carts," barked Jeff as Rose stood beside him.

"Mix'em if you got'em," said Davo as everyone settled into their buggies for the rule changes, schedule of events and other housekeeping details. As Jeff completed his list, everyone started positioning themselves for departure.

Jeff keyed the megaphone again and announced, "We've got Mizz Rose here to give us a blessing." He handed Rose the megaphone. Like a pro, she keyed the mic and sweetly said, "Let's all climb out of those carts and make your way up here to the front of the veranda for a bit of Sunday fellowship before we get started."

Everyone looked around and at each other as they moved toward the front as Rose had asked. Bewildered, they shuffled toward the front. No one had experienced this level of prayer at a golf tournament. Du smiled up at Rose and gave her a big "thumbs up" as he headed toward the back row of the assembled carts. Rose encouraged everyone to come up front, even prodding several by name.

"Come on, Billy, Odel. You know your wives are in the front row at Calgary this morning," she chided.

By the time she started her "sermonette," Du was already halfway down the back row, checking to make sure all clasps were flipped to their open position. He moved quickly but with no sense of urgency, even pausing to reposition several bags to assure they were in "launch" position. Rose was recognizing the member-guess committee by the time he hit the halfway mark. He flashed her a thumbs-up with a grin. Not an eye left Rose's shapely figure. Perfectly positioned 10 feet below her, the all-male crowd was mesmerized.

Du stopped long enough to give himself a pat on the back and celebrate his genius while taking a sip of his "Big Orange." He was a bona-fide genius and very shortly this mayhem would prove it. Rose continued recognizing the grounds crew, the greens superintendent, the club house staff, and gained another few minutes showering praise on Jeff. Finishing up, Du headed-up front to take his place in the assembly.

Rose promptly began adlibbing an invocation that would have made Billy Graham proud. Unnoticed by all but the five of us, Du enthusiastically joined the group in a loud "Amen" as she finished. He then started to chant "Rose ... Rose ... Rose ..." and glad-handed everyone within reach, making sure that all saw him. The property damage, fist fights, and overall carnage caused by this "bagging" would have certainly resulted in an ass-whipping for the culprit ... if he were found out.

As Rose regally descended from the veranda, she prepared herself for the 30-plus hugs she would receive from her throng of admirers. Doc, having positioned himself at the bottom step, extended his arm to steady her.

Hugging her way through her throng of subjects, Doc at her side, they all made their way thru the waiting booby-trapped buggies. Du was rubbing his hands together as Rose stepped into the cart. He was giddy as a child on Christmas morning. Kissing the giggling Rose on the cheek, he said, "Great job, partner. Every eye was on you. I got 'em all!"

He glanced over and winked at Davo, Chic, Beav and Jumbo.

Chapter XIX

Just then Jeff keyed the walkie-talkie and seconds later a shotgun blast echoed across the property. A cacophony of sounds exploded: electric carts jumped forward flipping golf bags full of clubs onto hoods of oncoming carts, or into the paths of slower buggies. Crashes resounded as drivers struggled to avoid flying bags of clubs and other carts. Yelling, cussing, and shaking fists, dismounting players narrowly avoided being run over. Everyone was trying to figure out what was happening and why. It was a disaster of biblical proportions, or in local terminology, "a real goat ropin'!"

Head pro and general manager Jeff Adams, who had personally assumed control of the tournament and the day's activities some 30 minutes earlier, observed the chaos that his carefully planned start of the final round had become. It had looked better on paper. He quickly put the bullhorn to his mouth, keyed the mic, and in the excitement of the moment forgot his carefully crafted "deep voice" and in a prepubescent, little-girl voice screamed,

"Stop, stop, please just stop! Pleeeazee just stop!"

The shrillness of that little-girl scream had the desired effect. Everyone looked up to see Jeff squeaking into the bullhorn from the veranda. His face red as a local tomato, Jeff's pageboy haircut bounced as he hopped up and down. As he surveyed the carnage from his vantage point, he noticed four carts that had not moved. Their occupants were wearing sunglasses and sipping cocktails. He could see them snickering at this catastrophe. A sickening feeling came over him at the realization the perpetrators of this disaster were right under his nose, enjoying their handiwork.

Panic turned to rage as Jeff rushed to confront them. Forgetting the steep decline of the circular stairway and his trademark cowboy books, his fury blinded him. He was going to "whup some ass!" Who knows what might have happened had he made it to them?

Alas his boot heel caught the next-to-the-bottom step, sending him flying, arms fully extended, bullhorn still clutched in his soon to be bleeding fingers, sliding head-first as if he were stealing second base.

By this time, everyone's attention had turned from the cart fiasco to the insane little man's screaming, headlong mad dash. A collective "ouch" arose from the crowd as Jeff belly-slid down the packed gravel path. Semi-conscious and bleeding from his palms, chest, thighs, and forehead, he laid there. Two club staffers arrived to pry the bullhorn from his grasp and half carry him into the locker-room.

In a concerned voice, Chic said, "I think the little guy is wound a bit tight. I thought I smelled alcohol on his breath this morning in the parking lot."

Du agreed. "Yep, me too," he said. "Let's get this mess cleaned up and moving. We're getting behind schedule." Du hollered, "Show's over, folks. Let's get those bags back on those carts. Remember to fasten the clasp," he added, grinning broadly, "and get out to your starting hole."

Du, like a traffic cop, directed the unraveling of the mess he had engineered. Chic had never seen him happier, his New World's Record in hand, sunglasses on, Big Orange in hand, directing traffic. The rest of the crew nodded approval in silent admiration.

Chapter XX

Fortunately, re-pairing the teams into flights had sep-
arated all four teams. Now paired with others, their
manners and golf etiquette were sure to improve. Rose
was still giggling, amused by her role in the "goat ropin'."

She now set out to add two new admirers to her
throng. As she teed up the ball at their first hole, Jimmy
gasped, "My Lord!" Du thought to himself, we've got
these guys.

Du and Rose were tied for the lead with Jimmy
and Will. Du could beat their best ball, especially with
nothing to concentrate on but golf. Rose was there at
his "beck and call" if things got close.

Beaver and the stylishly clad Doc were one shot
back in their flight and it all boiled down to how well
the Doc could hit his new loaner driver. His old one,
with the tiger head cover, still adorned the front of their
golf cart, a Masthead of sorts. At their opening hole,
Rick stepped out of his cart and asked, "Doc, isn't' that
your old driver?" pointing to the carts "Tiger Masthead."

"Yep," replied the Beav, "Doc hit his tee shot so hard on the fifth hole yesterday, the shaft popped! Looks good up there, don't it?"

Beav's needle would be the difference in this match. Doc nervously teed the ball up high and took a long but very timid swing at the ball. It popped straight up in the air, leaving a big white mark on the top of the head of his borrowed driver. Beaver leapt out of the cart, whipping his cap off his head, and tried to catch the ball like a center-fielder, basket-style. Just missing, he threw a big arm around the Doc's shoulder, escorting him back to the cart.

With his big blue eyes staring into the Doc's panic-stricken face, Beav said, "Doc, you're getting ready to have a big drink of voka!" The Doc, shaking his head, struggled to escape the bear hug as Beaver continued, "You can have it orally or rectally, your choice?"

The Doc froze, remembering yesterday's lessons, but quickly recovered and looking Beaver in the eye said, "Will you be joining me?"

"You are damn right I will!" Beaver replied, reaching into his bag for the handle of voka he always kept for "medicinal purposes," including snakebite and nerves.

Chic and Junior had played two holes before Chic unwittingly broke the cardinal rule, he'd learned the year before: no advice during a round. Junior had again driven his purple-striped Titleist into the trees. Chic's mind was still on the morning events when Junior asked, as he did before every shot, "How do I play this?"

Chic, having already sized up the shot as they approached, without looking up said, "Five-iron; align your shoulders and feet left of the tree and aim the club head at the flag. Eye on the ball and hit it solid."

Hearing a distinctive "whack!" Chic looked up to see Junior's ball start left of the tree and fade, quail-high, bouncing just in front of the green. The ball ran towards the flagstick, purple markings becoming more visible as it slowed, and settling one foot from the hole. Chic, shaking his head, took off his Oakley sunglasses, straining to confirm the results he'd seen.

Jumbo hopped off the back of the cart and was heading toward Junior, who was standing where he'd hit "the shot," arms raised in triumph. Their playing partners were out of their carts applauding as Jums reached Junior. His enthusiastic "low five" knocked Junior onto his back, his legs kicking in the air as he tried to return to his feet. The "lick" didn't even faze the still jubilant little man.

Jumbo quickly helped him to his feet, and Junior brushed himself off with all the dignity he could summon. Covered in pine straw, his hat knocked crooked, he hurried to the cart.

"Partner, that's a birdie 3, net eagle!" he exclaimed. Giving him a hug with a big grin, Chic said, "Yep, pards. Great shot!"

Then it began: Jumbo remounted the buggy, as Junior took his seat beside Chic and said, "You know, if you could give me a few lessons a week, I know I could win the Club Championship next spring!"

And Chic's round was shot. From that point on, he was consulted on every shot Junior hit: yardage, club, wind direction, alignment, grip, posture, and reading putts. Even Jumbo had had enough, heading off to find Davo and Paulie.

Davo and Paulie were kindred spirits. Both were football players at South Carolina and struggled to read the truth out of the Bible. Their liberalized handicaps were reflected in the pre-tournament pari-mutuel betting that made them 8-to-5 favorites. By the time Jumbo caught up with them, they were rolling along at 10-under par through eight holes and just hitting their stride.

With no chance of a bad lie, lost ball, or stymie in the rough, they were free-wheeling 260-yard tee shots, even on narrow holes. Neither of their opponents, who were keeping their score and supposed to be protecting the other competitors, made any attempt to discourage this onslaught of par. They wisely stayed out of their way.

After all, this was a gentlemen's game. On the fourteenth hole, Jumbo, Davo, and Paulie were searching for Paulie's errant tee shot. Jumbo asked, "What kind of ball are you playing, Paulie?"

Paulie replied, "Titleist, Number One."

Just before the five-minute time limit for looking

for a lost ball had expired, Paulie barked, "I got it! Right here out in the open, I don't know how we missed it. I walked over that area several times." Paulie hit a nice recovery onto the green and, after missing his eagle try, he tapped in for his net birdie.

On the fifteenth tee, as Paulie teed up his ball, Jums sidled up to Davo and handed him a Titleist Number One golf ball. "Found it under our cart when we pulled out of the woods back there. We must have parked the cart right on top of it," Jumbo explained.

Davo sheepishly smiled and accepted the ball. "What a coincidence, same brand and number as Paulie's ball," he said. "What are the odds?"

Chapter XXI

Jumbo decided he had seen enough of the pair's she-nanigans and figured a quick snack at the clubhouse buffet might be the ticket. Davo and Paulie drove him to the tenth green on their way to their second shot into the fifteenth hole. Jumbo happily made the short 125-yard walk to the clubhouse.

He thought over his options and quickly decided a double cheeseburger from the outside grill, washed down with a couple of coldbeers, might sustain him until the fish fry, some three hours away. The fish fry at Junior's lake house was always the finale of the Coon Hall Member Guest Weekend. Some called it the social event of the season. It was rumored that many members played in the tournament just to attend the fish fry.

None of this mattered to Jumbo as he took his first full "chomp" out of the man-sized burger. He decided he needed to take up golf, if for no other reason than the food. Jums wondered if there would be any snacks served at Junior's farm before the fish fry. Jumbo had inherited his father's ability to plan his next meal during the one he was eating.

Wondering why he was so hungry, he realized he'd eaten nothing since the four Hardee's steak biscuits he'd inhaled this morning, and it was lunchtime. As Jumbo took the last bite of his burger, he overheard a woman at the next table say, "they're posting the nine-hole scores for all of the flights."

Jumbo ambled over to the bar for a second coldbeer before heading over to the scoreboard to see where his teams stood thru nine holes. Twenty feet from the scoreboard, Jumbo stopped dead in his tracks. He quickly threw up a hand to stifle a snicker.

There in front of him stood Jeff Adams: page boy haircut, cowboy boots, and gauze bandages from head to toe, posting scores. Someone with medical training had cleaned and bound his wounds incurred during the "invocation." The three-inch wide band of gauze covering the scrape on his forehead reminded Jumbo of a sweatband he'd seen tennis pros on TV wear. The wounds on his forearms and palms of his hands were still oozing through the gauze.

Jeff's pants were frayed at both thighs down to his knees. As comical as all those battle scars were to Jumbo, the sight of the small circular band-aid on the tip of his nose and chin made Jums turn and retreat until he could compose himself. After five minutes and another coldbeer to fortify his funny bone, Jums made a second attempt to approach the scoreboard.

Jeff turned and, although he hadn't met Jumbo, recognized him from earlier in the day. He nodded to Jums. Jumbo raised his beer to the Pro and said, "Glad to see you're going to be okay, Pro." Jumbo, having had the "good cop-bad cop" routine played on him enough, knew he needed to be the "good cop." This wasn't over yet and the little man would be hunting some payback.

Checking each team's score through nine holes showed Davo and Paulie in control of their flight with a commanding three-shot lead. They would need to purposely blow a few shots on the last nine holes to keep from being tarred and feathered. Du and Rose also had a comfortable two-shot lead going into the final eight holes. Doc and Beav, like Chic and Junior, were tied with several other teams at the halfway point.

Jumbo decided to grab one coldbeer for the walk out to inform his teams of their positions. Davo and Paulie would be coming thru the eighteenth hole on their way to the finish. No need to warn them to apply the brakes. He walked from the sixteenth hole backwards in order to catch all three teams.

He caught Du and Rose on the fifteenth tee. Rose's waggle and wiggle distracted everyone except the tournament-seasoned Du. No problem there, they were still in control, three shots up with four holes to play.

Beav and Doc appeared in the fourteenth fairway. Beav had the Doc's alcohol level fine-tuned and they were cruising. They'd gained a shot on the flight leaders, their playing partners.

Once informed of this, Beaver decided to make use of his "go to" club down the stretch. His "mouth wedge" could be deadly from any position on the course, even from several fairways away.

As his opponent, Butch, addressed his second shot, Beav casually commented, "You really don't even notice that small pond to the left of this green. Hardly comes into play." Butch, who'd enjoyed the day until now, stepped away from his ball and started his pre-shot routine again.

"Yep, I pulled my shot yesterday just a little, and it ran right into that pond on the left. I made a damn six! Ruined my round," Beaver said, speaking to no one in particular.

Butch again stepped up to his second shot, maybe a little quicker than the first time, trying to get the shot off before Beav's commentary started again. Making his worst swing of the day, Butch pushed the ball well right of the Green, where it caromed off a shoulder into a thick bank of blackberry bushes.

As Beaver drove by on the way to his ball, he warned, "Careful in there, Butch. Rattlesnakes like black berries, too."

Jumbo spied Chic and Junior coming off the twelfth green and decided an "Easter egg hunt" in the "no-shoulders country" was not his idea of fun. Besides, with Beav's "mouth wedge" in play, he might better ske-daddle before things got ugly.

He met Chic as he walked onto the thirteenth tee. Chic looked exhausted, his head down and shoulders slumped. Jumbo asked, "How's it going?"

"Damnest thing I've ever seen!" Chic replied. "I've picked every one of his clubs, aimed him on every shot, read every putt and answered every golf question imag-inable. Don't get me wrong, he's a great guy, but he's on my last nerve. I feel like I've been beat with a stick. Not even 'Mr. Booze' is helping at this point. How's every-one else doing?"

"The others are either leading or close," Jumbo an-swered. "How about you guys?" expecting a bad report.

"Unbelievably, we're tied for the lead," Chic said. "Junior and I have been ham-and-egging it pretty well. It's just a question of survival at this point: mine. Watch."

As Chic pointed at Junior on the tee, who was chat-tering as he set up.

"Punkin, does this look okay?" Junior asked.

"Great!" sighed an exasperated Chic.

Junior hit a perfect shot down the fairway, picked up his tee and ambled over to them. "How you do-ing, Punkin?" he said to Jumbo. Junior called everyone Punkin. Remembering names, as with golf tips, was not his strong point.

"Good, Junior. Nice tee ball," Jumbo said.

Turning to Chic, Junior asked him, with a perplexed look on his face, "Do you inhale or exhale on your backswing?"

"I'm not sure, Junior," Chic barked. "Get in the cart. Jums, hop on!" He was eager to get this round, over regardless of the outcome.

Chapter XXII

They dropped Jumbo within 100 yards of the clubhouse and continued on Chic's quest for the last hole and relief. Jums climbed up the stairs to the scoring area and found himself in a dilemma: coldbeer or burger?

Mid-ponder, Jumbo looked up to see Jeff coming his way. He looked like a cross between a mummy and a Revolutionary war drum and fife corps reenacter. Limping up to Jums, Jeff stuck out a gauze wrapped hand and said, "Hi, I'm Jeff Adams, head pro and general manager here at Calhoun Country Club. I don't believe we've met."

Jums, about twice Jeff's size, gently shook his hand and said, "Hi Jeff, I'm James, the younger brother; everyone calls me Jumbo."

"How about a beer, Jumbo?" asked Jeff.

"Great, don't mind if I do," Jumbo said. Jeff went to the bar to order him a beer. "What's your poison, Jumbo?" he asked

"Buttweiser," Jumbo replied.

Handing him the cold beer, Jeff asked, "You got a minute to talk?" Cautiously, his mind racing, Jumbo said, "Sure, Jeff," anticipating trouble.

Jeff made his way to an unoccupied table at the corner of the patio. Sitting down, he pulled out a chair for Jumbo.

"So, you're the chauffeur today?" Jeff said with a smile. "Just kidding, although you're a big improvement; that stunt yesterday almost got me fired. Lots of folks around here still have old-fashioned ideas about that sort of thing."

"I'd say they need to get with the times," Jumbo replied, smiling innocently.

"Oh, they know that, but they consider this little patch of ground a place where they can honor the old ways and their ancestors," Jeff said. "Can I ask you a question, Jumbo? Why do those guys hate me so much? They treat me like their little bitch."

"Oh now, Jeff they'd never call you that … to your face," Jumbo said, turning his head and covering his mouth as his voice trailed off.

"What?" Jeff said, straining to hear.

"Well, it would be, uh, like a term of endearment," Jumbo said. "Everyone had a nickname. Besides, it's not you, it's the authority you represent. Just ignore them. I wasn't real happy with 'Jumbo' when they hung that on me, but resisting is only going to make it worse."

"So, when 72 golf bags go flipping off the backs of 36 golf carts at the start of the club's premier event, I'm supposed to ignore it?" Jeff said, more than a little hot.

Jumbo rocked back in his chair, his eyes opened wide, as he gave the mini-pro the once over. "Hey pro, you asked me and I'm trying to help. Help me, help you."

"You're right. Go ahead," Jeff said, dropping his head.

"That circus stunt you pulled coming off the veranda, headfirst, made you look like a fool in front of the entire club and their guests," Jumbo continued. Jeff's head dropped further.

"How'd that work out for you?" Jumbo asked. "What were you going to do once you got to them? Whip the four of them", and me"?

Jeff's head hit the table. He snapped up, yelling, "Ouch!"

"You gave them exactly what they were looking for. Hell more than they were looking for," Jumbo added. Jeff held up his bandaged hand. "Stop," he said. "I get it, I get it!"

"Maybe a little chuckle when they're provoking you," Jumbo said. "Just don't for God's sake get into a verbal altercation with any one of them. Take it from me; they are professional raconteurs and agitators. You're not their first victim and you won't be their last. Like a pack of wolves".

"Try and stay out of their way, if you can do that for the rest of the day, and you may survive," Jumbo added. "You realize your most prominent members love us. Paulie, Rose, Junior, and at his request, we're using the club president's private parking space."

"Damn, Jumbo, when you explain it like that, I look like a fool," Jeff said woefully.

"Imbecile," Jumbo corrected. "Just stay out of their way and smile at everything they say or do."

"I appreciate you helping me, Jumbo," Jeff said. Jumbo toasted the little pro as he limped away, and said to himself, "We'll see."

Chapter XXIII

The teams were finishing as Jumbo finished his Buttweiser. He headed out to the parking lot to open the Suburban. One of the advantages of a shotgun start was in addition to starting at the same time, everyone finished at the same time. Traditionally at Coon Hall's Member-Guest, all scorecards were turned in for the staff to total up, apply handicaps, play off ties on the cards, and declare flight and parimutuel winners. The presentation of trophies, awards, and cash would be made prior to the fish fry during the cocktail hour at Junior's lake house.

A special setting this time of year, Junior's lake house sat at the bottom of a small bluff near a spillway that controlled the water level of 200 Acre Lake. Large stones had been added to the spillway to give it the look and sound of a babbling brook. The cottage sat in a small grove of pines, cedars, azaleas and live oaks. Surrounded by fertile fields, whose planting had become very scientific, access to the cottage was down a renowned live-oak-lined lane. In addition to irrigation, the lake was used for hunting, fishing, boating, swimming, and relaxation. An enormous deck tied the cottage to the boat house and dock.

Generations of planters had each contributed to this haven. The club staff had been setting up for 200-plus guests since Friday. Players, wives, and guests would be attending the "social event of the season."

Jumbo dutifully helped load clubs into the back of the Suburban as one by one, all four teams finished. Du and Rose were beaming and celebrating what they figured was a victory. Rose looked fresh as a daisy and Du cool as a cucumber as they headed to the clubhouse to turn in their scorecard. Jumbo reminded them, "Twenty minutes to departure for Junior's Plantation."

Next to arrive were Davo and Paulie, in a heated discussion as to what score they would need to win, without looking like a couple of thieves. Davo argued that a self-imposed two-shot penalty should do the trick.

"Paulie, you improperly dropped that ball on the fourth hole, disqualifying your birdie three, making my bogey five count, and there you go," Davo said. "Twenty-two under should do it quite nicely."

"Yep," Paulie agreed, "anyone beating that score is definitely a crook."

Jumbo reminded them of the 15-minute departure. Up drove Beav and the Doc, having finished with seven straight birdies and a 17-under par round.

"Doc, old buddy, old pal, that was a great round," said Beav as he threw a "meat hook" arm around the Doc's newly purchased cotton shirt.

"Couldn't have done it without your coaching, Beav," Doc said, squirming as he tried to keep his new outfit unruffled

Just then Chic and Junior skidded up, Chic half out of the cart before it stopped.

"Whew, what a round!" he exclaimed. "Punkin's birdie at the last may have just gotten us into the money," Chic said, mimicking Junior's speech.

He handed Beav their scorecard. "How 'bout turn this in for us and get back here PDQ," Chic said. "Junior, didn't you say you needed to call the house and let them know we're heading that way? I need a shower and a double transfusion. Come on, chop- chop, let's get at it; places to go, things to do, people to meet."

Beav rolled his eyes. "Chill out, bro," he said, recognizing the symptoms of "The Chics," a hyperactive state his older brother slipped into when he had many moving parts running. This situation qualified; Beaver had to admit.

"Beav, you didn't leave that firecracker in that hot truck, did you?" Chic asked.

"Nope. Got it right here in my golf bag with the cooler pressed up against it," Beaver replied.

"Good thinking," Chic said, shaking his head at the thought of how this would end.

Junior perked up. "You guys got a firecracker?"

Beaver caught himself. "Yeah, sort of a M-80 left over from the Fourth of July," he said. "I guess we could surprise everyone at the party."

"Great! We've never had fireworks at the finale," Junior said.

Chic and the Beaver smirked at each other, knowing what the half stick of dynamite could do.

Just then Paulie and Rose appeared from the club house. "I just called Dolly and told her we're on the way," she said. Junior snapped to attention; he'd invited five strangers to the house – her house – for showers, cocktails, appetizers and a tour of the plantation. Now he'd been caught yucking it up in the parking lot instead of rushing home to help as he'd been instructed to do that very morning.

Not Junior's first offense, this was exactly the sort of thing that had kept his "young ass" in the doghouse for weeks over their marriage. Dolly was responsible for their social status in the community. A stern taskmaster, she was not afraid to jerk Junior's apron strings in public. Dolly kept Junior on a short leash, as he tended to be very social.

That fate was running through Junior's brain as he headed toward his truck at a full trot, yelling back over his shoulder, "Y'all give me a 10-minute head start."

Chapter XXIV

Paulie, addressing the amused group, announced, "Mount up, guys, and follow me, I'll show you my deer club, 'Horney.' It's not out of the way and may just give Junior the time he'll need to talk his way out of this."

The small log cabin had been in Rose's ex-husband's family for years. As part of her divorce settlement, Rose was grudgingly awarded the 75-acre tract that bordered the Congaree Swamp to the southeast. The deer hunting, fishing and boar hunting were excellent. A good crop of acorns would assure a good summer duck season.

After their marriage, Paulie, staking his claim as a local, was trying to erase his carpetbagger status. He had added a large, screened porch, maple floors, stainless steel appliances, a hot tub and something no transplanted Yankee could live without in the South – two tons of central air conditioning, replacing a couple of window units. Calhoun County's scorching summer could "burn the ass off of the fire chief," in local slang.

Paulie turned down a long tree-lined dirt road, parking at the front porch. Jumbo parked the Suburban behind Paulie's black Cadillac El Dorado. Rose exited the Caddy, complaining the place was a mess. Paulie stepped out and up slowly, like a feudal lord, welcoming his royal visitors and knowing everyone in Columbia would now get a full description of his "hunt club." Stepping into the two-story great room, everyone's attention went to the large stone fireplace. An eight-foot-wide hearth fronted a four-foot-tall firebox.

"I have the wood specially cut for this fireplace. It heats the whole cabin, even in January," Paulie said. The walls were adorned with every species of bird, animal, or fish native to the area. Just above the fireplace mantel was a massive twelve-point buck.

Davo, remembering the story of Paulie's first hunting trip in Calhoun County, stopped Paulie mid-sentence and asked, "Is that the deer you killed when you first learned to shoot a 30-06?"

"Uh," Paulie stammered, clearing his throat, "no, uh. . . no." He'd been caught off guard. Du, smelling blood in the water, said, "Come on, Davo, tell us the story. . ."

Paulie, now moving quickly through the tour, said quickly, "Nothing to tell, just an accident."

"Come on, Paulie, you almost lost that eye, it was black, blue, yellow and green for a month," Davo said, nudging Du.

"Yeah, Paulie," chimed in Du. "Tell us the story."

"Nothing to tell, God-damn it!" Paulie shouted. "I got my eye too close to the scope and when I pulled the trigger, it kicked back up into my eye. First time I ever, shot a rifle. What's so funny about that? Happens all the time."

Rose stepped in to save him as she often did. "Paulie, don't you think we should get going?" she said.

"Hmmm," Paulie said, clearing his throat. "Yeah, let's get moving," he said, still steaming from Davo's needle.

Everyone piled into the two vehicles for the short ride to Junior's farm. Paulie was still grumbling at being "ridiculed" in his own fiefdom. Rose rolled her eyes. The Suburban's occupants were rehashing Davo's lampooning of Paulie. Sensitivity was not a highly prized trait in this clan. If you were thin-skinned this probably wasn't the place for you. . . and everyone knew it.

In fact, especially when they were involved in a "goat rodeo," their mission statements were, "Ridicule is the sincerest form of flattery," and "If you can't eat it or drink it . . . tear it up." This was a goat rodeo of the third kind: "No fences."

Chapter XXV

The giggling stopped as the two vehicles turned off the main road into a magnificent brick-pillared entrance adorned with two limestone sculpted lions on each side of the gate and gas lanterns atop the pillars. Down the customary live oak-lined entrance, they could just make out a large fountain. As they eased down the white gravel lane, the shenanigans were replaced with a silence of awe.

"You sure you're in the right place?" cracked Davo.

Jumbo snapped, "I'm following Paulie, remember?"

To their right, a series of golf flags appeared on a manicured lawn. The left side of the entrance past the oaks looked to be an equestrian training area complete with gates, jumps and a track around the perimeter. Even Du seemed impressed as he flicked his sunglasses to the bridge of his nose for a better look.

"Chic, did you know Junior was this wealthy?" he asked.

"I met him a year ago, and have heard him talk

about the farm, but I had no idea it was anything like this." Chic said in a whisper. "You've been around him; he's not trying to impress anyone."

"Anyone but you," Beav said. "Maybe you ought to slide over here and give him a few lessons on long, relaxing weekends. Might be a good gig."

Jumbo followed Paulie's El Dorado around the fountain and brought the Suburban to a stop. Everyone reverently disembarked at the front of the massive Greek Revival, six-column colonial plantation mansion.

"I'd have felt more comfortable showing up here in the Rolls," Du quipped, breaking the tension for a moment. The "crunching" of the freshly raked white gravel under their feet obscured the creaking of the massive front door opening. Transfixed by the impressive grandeur, Dolly's southern drawl jolted them from their trance-like state.

"Welcome to 'Bon Tarra.' Y'all come on in, it's so nice to have you here," cooed the perfectly coiffed Dolly. Resplendent in a pink sundress, there was no question "Miss Dolly" was the true "Master" of this house. Rose ascended the eight granite steps up to the portico and received a familiar embrace.

Paulie obediently followed his wife and was similarly received. The three then turned, forming an impromptu receiving line. Paulie looked down on the visitors and gave a quick nod of his head, signaling it was time to be received. Hats came off and bellies were sucked in. What primping and straightening that could be done was done.

Sunglasses still hanging on the bridge of his nose, Du raised his eyebrows as if to say, "Oh brother." One by one, they started their ascent, when there was a commotion from inside the house. Seconds later, a small muscular gentleman in a orange and white starched gingham shirt, pressed khakis and new Topsiders, took up a position at the end of the receiving line. He resembled Junior. Heads cocked and strained as all except Chic tried to identify this interloper.

Chic was last in line, next to Du. Although he'd never seen Junior wearing "Clemson Orange," instinctively he knew he must own some. How many 5-foot-3, heavily freckled redheads could be at Junior's home? Chic didn't want to follow that line of thought and turned his attention to the progress of the procession.

The line moved slowly up the steps. Acting as a royal footman, Paulie politely introduced Dolly to her guests, using Christian names: Bryan instead of Beaver, James instead of Jumbo. Everyone was mightily impressed at Paulie's performance, none more than Rose at his right elbow.

Decorum broke down as each guest gave Rose her customary hug. Never schooled in the European embrace, each did manage a scaled-back, less familiar hug for Dolly. Recognizing Junior as the mystery host, decorum left them. Beaver, first in line, clapped Junior on the back so hard, he spilled a swallow of his mint julep out of his silver cup.

Beaver exclaimed, "Junior, old panther, you've been holding out on us; beautiful place." He quickly moved forward, spying a silver tray of mint juleps, and helped himself to a cup. As he struggled to get a swallow without consuming the fresh mint garnish, Minnie, who ran the house for Ms. Dolly, stepped in.

"Just push it down into the drink, several sprigs are already "muddled" into the bottom so you ain't hurtin' nothin'," she said. Beaver thanked her and joined Jumbo in the two-story entry. Davo and Du moved respectfully into the vast entry hall.

Chic, introduced as Charles, took Dolly's hand, and said, "Mrs. …"

"Stop right there, young man," she said. "I can see you know your manners but please call me Dolly. Junior has told me so much about you, I feel as if I know you."

"Ok, Dolly, thank you so much for inviting us to your gorgeous home," Chic said. "It's truly a privilege to be here."

"We'll have a chance to talk later; for now, we're glad to have you here," Dolly purred.

Quickly shaking Paulie's hand and giving Rose a peck on the check, Chic moved to Junior. Shaking his hand, Chic grabbed Junior's right elbow with his left hand and pulled him into his chest.

"Damn, pardner, this is some place," he said. "You've

got your own practice range, too."

"I told you I just needed some lessons from you," Junior said, stepping back from the hug.

"We'll work that out," Chic replied as he sought out a mint julep.

Junior followed him over to where Minnie stood holding the silver tray with four mint juleps on it. "Fresh mint grows out back at the north wall of the foundation," he said. "That makes all the difference. I use rye whiskey instead of bourbon; makes a smoother drink. I can give you the recipe and a sprig or two of mint to plant. That mint has been growing there since I was a boy..."

Chic cut him off and whispered, "Maybe later. What I really need now is a shower and a change of clothes. By the way, you look really sharp. Never seen you in orange before."

"It was a gift," Junior said.

"Well, it looks great. . . and you can hunt quail in it, or pick up trash on the side of the road," Chic said with a chuckle.

"Come on," Junior said, chuckling himself. "I'll show you the guest room. You can clean up and change there. The others can use the bunkhouse in the back yard. I got to take care of my pardner."

"Thanks, pardner," Chic said, nodding. "How about tell those reprobates to get ready, and then show them to the bunkhouse. It's just over an hour to the party and we're all looking forward to a tour of the farm. You're still planning to take us, right?"

"The 'Money Maker' is all gassed up and ready to go," Junior said. "I just need to get my clubs and shoes out of the back. I had a couple of bales of fresh hay put into the bed so two guys could ride back there."

"'Money Maker'; is that like Betsy, a pet name for your truck?"

"Well yeah, but that's the name Ford used to market it in 1955," Junior said. "It's actually a 1955 F100 pick-up. All original parts, never restored, runs like a sewing machine."

Chic closed the guest room door. A mint julep with rye whiskey and fresh sprigs of home-grown, 50-year-old mint, a shower, and some fresh clothes, would make a new man out of him and ready for the farm tour.

Twenty minutes later, they found themselves assembled in the state-of-the-art, newly renovated kitchen. Dolly's one-year project had brought together the finest designers and most talented craftsman from Charleston to shoehorn this culinary palace into the historic mansion. Museum-quality art was carefully placed throughout the white marble canvas. Stainless appliances, copper cookware and indirect lighting gave the kitchen a laboratory feeling. The custom-made, hanging brushed-copper pot rack with down lights highlighted the copper vein in the expansive white marble island.

Dolly's pride was tempered by the fact Minnie and

the girls preferred the detached cookhouse for meal preparation. This kitchen, now used for staging meals, had become the gathering area for guests as most kitchens do. After several minutes of small talk, Junior appeared, purple cap atop his red hair. Now all was right with the world. Fresh drinks in hand, everyone filed out to board the Money Maker, with Junior arranging the seating,

Chapter XXVI

"Chic, you and Jumbo hop in the back, that hay is really comfortable," Junior said. "Davo, you're next to me. Du, you're in the middle; Beav, window seat, shotgun."

In true Three Stooges fashion, the group saluted, milled around bumping into each other, before climbing into the big, roomy pickup. Beav, last to board, tossed his black backpack onto the floorboard. Du and Davo flinched as it tumbled onto the floor at their feet. Beaver entered with raised eyebrows, chin tucked and a big grin on his face.

"Thought I'd forgotten," he said, laughing.

Junior stepped out to make sure Chic and Jumbo were comfortable. Du snickered, "I bet you don't have matches and this old buggy don't have a light."

"Dumbass, there's no fuse on this thing," Beav said. "You strike it like a road flare."

"Yeah, cheesedick, Beav's got this all under control, he's a professional," Davo said as Junior hopped back in and fired up the truck.

Off they went, on a 30-minute tour. What could go wrong? Alcohol and dynamite? Chic anticipated a bad outcome.

First stop was the barn, about 500 yards from the house. It was a massive structure and according to local lore sat on the highest point in the county. As the group climbed the cypress-hewn stairway to the loft, Junior told stories of how his grandfather had watched the smoke rise from Columbia as Sherman's troops burned the capital in February 1865. From the loft, most of the 2,000-acre farm was visible, including the lake house that was already buzzing with activity.

Chic, already aching from the quarter-mile ride from the house to the barn, caught Junior's eye, tapped his watch and said, "Junior, you weren't kidding when you said the Money Maker hadn't been restored. Those stocks have got to be at least 25 years old. Let's take a look at the Lincoln and head over to the party to collect our loot."

Jumbo piped up. "I've been waiting all day for those fried bream and hush-puppies."

Once downstairs, Junior led everyone to a corner of the original structure. As they gathered, Junior flipped on a large florescent light. The flickering light gradually revealed a 1965 White Lincoln Continental Mark II. The black leather interior and white exterior were pristine. Beaver reverently opened the driver's door and exclaimed, "Hey the keys are in it, how about if I . . . "

"Nope, no, absolutely not, forget about it, no frigging way!" Chic barked.

"Yeah, Beav, you remember the joyride you took in Mom's Crown Vic that ended with it upside down on the railroad track, on fire, don't cha?" Davo said.

Everyone was belly-laughing as Beaver, with a hurt look on his face, said, "You guys don't forget 'nuttin'. That was a couple of years ago."

"Beav, let me remind you, this car is irreplaceable, and there is 'no education in the second kick of a mule'," Chic chided him.

"But think how cool we'd look pulling up to the party in this carriage?" Beaver pleaded.

"I thought you already had that planned," Chic said.

"Well, I guess," muttered Beaver, closing the door and helping Junior replace the cover.

Everyone piled back into the Money Maker for the ride to the lake house. Lake Lane meandered for a half-mile down to the lake house from the barn's perch. The lane was now a sunken dirt road bordered by hedge-rows. The hedgerows were a feature Junior's father had brought back from Normandy, having been there days after the D-Day invasion. They served as drainage ditch-es and windbreaks preventing valuable topsoil from be-ing washed or blown away.

Fertile fields could be glimpsed thru breaks in the hedgerows on both sides of the lane. Two hundred yards to the left, the field followed the shoreline of the lake and gradually descended to the lake house. The last 75 yards had been graded and benched into a terraced amphitheater. The natural-grassed amphitheater overlooked the large deck. At this point, the contoured bank of the lake provided a 20-foot drop, perfect for the rope swing hanging from a lone live oak.

The large oak also provided shade to the deck from the setting sun. Furrows were plowed perpendicular to the lake and lane, preventing blowing dust and erosion.

In the middle of his running commentary, without warning, Junior slammed on the brakes and whipped the pickup's large steering wheel to the left. Everyone lurched forward and to the right. Jumbo and Chic were thrown off their hay bales. Had the bed of the antique F100 not been so wide and deep, they would have been ejected.

"What the fu…..?" came a collective grown. Junior had turned quickly into a gap in the hedgerow used by combines and plows.

"Hey, I got to show ya'll a ride my grandchildren love," Junior crowed as he continued 50 yards into the field. The tires of the pickup fit nicely into the furrows like grooves. Just as everyone was repositioned, he slammed on the brakes and jerked the wheel to the right, jolting them again.

"Junior, dammit, that's about enough," growled Du.

"We're gonna ride the weezes," cried Junior as he hit the gas. Now the ride was across the plowed furrows, wash-boarding the occupants of the antique Ford. As the speed increased, so did the volatility of the ride. Heads hit the roof and asses banged the worn bench seat. Screams of "stop!" did nothing as Junior gleefully continued. The ride in the back, not nearly as luxurious as the cab, had Jumbo and Chic hanging on for dear life, while they slapped the roof and back windows screaming, "STOP"!

Davo tried pulling Junior's foot off the gas pedal while Du tried to wrestle the steering wheel from his grasp. After what seemed like an eternity, they bounced to a stop. The truck emptied as a dust cloud enveloped the addled occupants.

"Damn, Junior, I wouldn't beat a rented mule like that," hollered Davo, coughing up a mouthful of dust. Chic chimed in, "I've ridden mechanical bulls that were smoother!"

"My grandkids love it," Junior said, sounding confused. "As we bounce up and down over the furrows, they yell 'wee, wee.'"

"Yeah, but they weigh thirty pounds and are four feet tall," Du yelled, disgusted. "I'll bet you don't drive 30 miles an hour, either."

Beav, ever the fashion plate, found himself 15 feet from the Money Maker in a cloud of dust. As he cleaned the debris from his hand-picked "party duds," the cloud of dust began to settle. Below him, some two hundred yards in the distance, the Lake House and its festivities appeared. At that moment, his plan came to him fully formed. He continued brushing the fine layer of dust from his French blue linen shirt as he strolled over to where others gathered, planning his presentation along the way.

Beav's attitude was always positive and a big part of his appeal to both men and women alike. "Hey Cheesers (short for Cheesedicks)," he said, "I've come up with a stroke of genius!" Du flicked his RayBans down to the tip of his nose and gave Davo a raised eyebrow doubtful look.

"OK, hot shot, let's hear it," said Davo. Beaver continued nonchalantly, whisking the dust from his flax-colored linen pants as he casually straightened himself and turned in the direction of Junior's Lake House. By now the festive assembly could be clearly seen from their vantage point. From this distance with the Sun at their back, it was doubtful anyone at the Party would even notice the truck or the six of them at the top of the field.

Beaver started laying out his plan, slowly and calmly at first. "Same seating as before: Junior at the wheel, Davo and Du in the middle, me riding shotgun; Chic and Jumbo in the back on the hay bales," he began.

"Oops! Hold it right there: no way, no how, no sir," Chic interrupted. "I'm not getting back in that 'bucking bronc'! How about you, Jumbo?"

" I've been saving myself for those fried bream and hushpuppies," Jums said, licking his lips.

"Exactly!" Chic said, making clear he wanted no part of the looming disaster he anticipated. "Junior can drop Jumbo and me off at the front of the cottage un-noticed, and then come back up the lane to pick you guys up." Chic slid under the wheel, directing Junior and Jumbo to follow. "We'll make sure you've got an au-dience watching the finale. So good luck and be careful," he said, starting the truck.

The occupants of the Money Maker were nervously silent during the short ride down the lane to the cottage. The old pickup pulled up to the front entrance unob-served as Chic shifted into neutral and set the parking brake. As he exited, Junior slid under the wheel. Jumbo joined Chic at the front steps, and they gave Junior an informal salute as he slipped the truck into gear, released the brake and headed back up the lane. With a hesitant wave he was gone.

In Junior's absence, the "brain trust" had mixed cocktails from the cooler Du had liberated as the truck pulled away. The Grand Finale had been carefully planned and revised by the time Junior returned. All that was left was to fill Junior in on the "revised" plan, which avoided mentioning the stick of dynamite, substituting the term "firecracker" in its place. Sort of like calling a tidal wave a "ripple."

The "brain trust" had reasoned a panicky driver was not a good thing – unusually clear thinking from this group, who had consumed their first sip of voka before 8 that morning.

Junior slowly positioned the Money Maker next to the cooler, trying not to stir up another cloud of dust. He carefully aimed it across the furrows towards the Lake House, ready for departure. Hopping out, Junior grabbed a coldbeer from the cooler and proceeded to chugalug it, knocking the dust from his throat. Beav started the briefing.

"OK, we're going to head straight down the field towards the Lake House – SLOWLY, Junior," he added. "Just before the bottom terrace, I'm going to strike the … oops, light the firecracker. I'll throw it to the bottom of the terrace, and you hit the brakes and turn the wheel hard over, and skid sideways to a stop just in front of the firecracker. There will be a loud blast followed by a cloud of dust and smoke. We'll all hop out, raise our arms and wait for the dust to clear."

"Then what?" asked Junior.

"Then we accept the cheering from the crowd on the deck," Beav said. "It will be the finest Grand Finale in the history of the Coon Hall Member Guest." He paused, then said, "One last thing: a toast to our mission!"

"Kind of like the kamikaze pilots?" Du suggested.

"Oh, that's appropriate enough. Anyone got sake?" Davo snickered.

Beav resumed his speech while glaring at Du and Davo. "Everyone got a drink?" he asked. Junior hurriedly tossed his empty into the Money Maker's bed and extracted another coldbeer from the cooler. Beaver raised his cup, motioning for all to join him. "Skol!" he shouted and raised his cup to his mouth.

Noticing no one was following his lead, he stopped. "What's wrong?" he asked. Du looked at Davo and said, "I thought it was "Banzai!"

"Banzai, Skol, what's the difference? He's on a roll," Davo said, laughing. "Down the hatch!"

The drinks were downed. "OK, let's go!" shouted a fully committed Junior, as they piled into the truck: same seating with Junior piloting, Davo, Du, and Beav in the shotgun position/passenger window. "Not too fast now Junior, "warned the Beav".

Off they went. It was a beautiful late summer afternoon, an hour until sunset. What could go wrong? Alcohol, dynamite, and two hundred and fifty witnesses.

Down at the lake house, Chic was standing at the bar, ordering a Big Orange in honor of his friend Du. Watching the machinelike efficiency that Jumbo used to devour fried bream was like watching an industrial tree thrasher at work: fish in, bones and fins out. Jumbo had consumed three in about four minutes. Just hitting his stride, Jums was about to make short work of a fourth bream when Chic walked over and tapped him on the shoulder, careful not to get his fingers near Jumbo's mouth.

"Come on, it won't be long now," Chic said as he made his way to the edge of the deck nearest the amphitheater. Every couple of feet, Chic was asked, "Where are the guys?" Big Orange in his right hand, Chic pointed his left hand towards the Lone Oak just above the deck at the bottom of the field.

Just then, the Money Maker appeared at the top of the hill, the setting sun and the trailing dust silhouetting the big pickup. Jumbo joined him and on cue bent down behind Chic and yelled at the top of his lungs: "GREAT GODFREY DAMN!!!"

A hundred guests turned quickly to see what all the commotion was about, and the rest turned to see what they were looking at. Now every eye was on the truck jumping, bumping, and bouncing toward them, dust trail following.

In the truck, Beav leaned down to retrieve the device. Carefully concealing the 12-inch tube from Junior, Beaver removed the cap. Once the dangling cord was yanked, the fuse would burn intensely for five seconds, causing a loud screaming and whistling, simulating an incoming artillery shell. At the end of five seconds would come the blast, equivalent to a half stick of dynamite.

"OK, Junior: 40 yards to the terrace, keep it slow and easy," directed the Beav as he prepared to yank the cord. Junior, expecting to see an M-80 firecracker, glanced over and caught a glimpse of the stick of dynamite. A terror-stricken look came over his face, and he unwittingly accelerated.

Beaver yanked the cord and the fuse ignited, burning hotly as he fully extended his arm out the open window. "Twenty yards to the bottom!" Du shouted.

"Slow down Junior," the Beav commanded, struggling with the increasingly rough ride. "Fifteen yards!" Du yelled, continuing the countdown, as Beaver cocked his arm all the way back for the throw.

Then ... BANG! The whole truck shuddered as it violently hit bottom, tossing everyone into the air. Beav snatched his empty hand back into the cab as they landed with a loud "thud!" Dazed and confused, Davo looked to his right at Du, who was rubbing the top of his head. He saw Beav sitting Zombie-like in his seat, his eyes wide shut, hands by his sides. Looking past Du, Davo suddenly shouted, "Where is it?!"

The panic-stricken Beav replied unevenly, "In the truck....I think."

"Oh SHIT! It's in the truck!" Davo screamed.

Du joined in screaming, but his voice was drowned

out by a high-pitched whistling coming from just be-hind them, in the bed of the truck. At the wheel, recov-ering from the Money Maker bottoming out, Junior had figured out this was no firecracker. The hotly burning fuse set the hay in the back of the truck on fire. The occupants' yelling increased and turned into squealing.

"I'm going to put her into the Lake!" Junior shout-ed, turning the wheel hard to the left.

From the deck, Chic, Jumbo and several hundred revelers watched intently as the big truck jumped wild-ly between furrows, bouncing its passengers around like rag dolls. Some 40 yards above the deck, after a par-ticularly spectacular jump, the antique truck started a turn towards the lake. As the now flaming truck turned broadside to the deck, a high-pitched whistle turned into a screech.

A bright flash followed by an excruciatingly loud blast shocked the crowd below. Drinks spilled, wom-en screamed, and every eye watched breathlessly as the flaming pickup headed towards the Lone Oak and a 20-foot plunge into the lake.

The blast blew out the back window of the truck, allowing flaming hay to dance into the cab. Stunned but conscious, Junior instinctively turned the flaming pickup towards the Lake where he intended to extinguish the fire. Covered in glass, stunned, and half deaf, Davo, Du, and the Beav knew the plunge would probably kill them.

Remembering the futility of trying to wrestle the wheel from Junior, Davo threw a meat-hook forearm around Junior's thick, freckled neck. Du struggled to pull Junior's muscular leg off the accelerator. Beaver tried to reach the gearstick to knock the truck out of gear. The life-or-death struggle continued until Junior finally lost consciousness,15 yards from the Oak.

After pulling his leg off the gas pedal, Du reached up and switched off the engine. The Money Maker, now engulfed in flames, lurched twice and died under the Live Oak. Smoke billowed from the truck, partially obscuring the heroic efforts of the survivors from the awe-struck crowd below.

Davo reached over Junior's limp body and opened the door, shoving the two of them out, tumbling onto the ground. Du and the Beav performed a similar ejection on the other side of the flaming pickup. Davo dragged Junior over to the Oak and propped him up against the trunk, while Du and the Beav circled the truck. Finding a pitchfork attached just behind the cab, they raked the flaming bales of straw harmlessly onto the plowed ground.

Davo had nearly revived Junior when Du and the Beav joined them under the Oak. As the smoke and dust began to clear, Junior was getting to his feet.

On the deck 60 feet below, some 200 revelers had witnessed the spectacle. Dumbfounded, they stood open-mouthed as the four survivors gathered under the Live Oak next to the smoldering bales of hay and the scorched Money Maker.

Chic elbowed Jumbo and sat his Big Orange on the top rail of the deck. Pointing his chin at the four survivors under the Oak, Chic started clapping, motioning Jumbo to join in. As the clapping spread throughout the crowd, Davo clasped Junior's hand and raised it into the air like a victorious prizefighter.

Du and the Beav joined them, and the four survivors stood there, clasped hands raised into the air, to accept their ovation for the damnedest Coon Hall Member Guest Finale anyone could remember. And the ovation continued.......

THE END

GLOSSARY

Albatross - Three under par on one hole. 2 on a par 5. Ace on a par 4.

Ace- Hole in one shot

Birdie - One shot less than par on a hole

Big Orange - Voka and soda often equal parts. Garnished with a "Big Orange slice" when possible.

Buttweiser- Budweiser in redneck slang

Abe Lincoln - Amaretto and Cognac. Brandy may be substituted. Sweeten to taste with Amaretto. It will "set you free"! Better "Duck Hunting" than playing golf.

Bogie - One shot over par on a hole

Cape Cod Cooler - 2 oz. Voka 3 oz. cranberry juice Shaken. Good for urinary tract infections. If you can't say it three times quickly, you don't need another.

ColdBeer - Southern for Cold Beer The "D" in beer may be omitted. Not to be used above the Mason Dixon Line.

Voka - Vodka

V 3 - Not the German Rocket that terrorized London but responsible for lots of terror. Voka Voka Voka different brands please.

Press- Start a new bet.

Handle - A 1.75 liter bottle of liquor. Formerly a half gallon. It has a handle. 59.8 oz. 39- 1.5 oz shots.

18 Holes - In Scotland where Golf began, a bottle of Scotch contained 18- 1.5 oz shots.

Dormie- in match play one team or player must win the remaining holes in order to tie their opponent.

Eagle- Two under par on one hole

Double Eagle- 3 under par on one hole. Albatross is also three under par on one hole. Continuation of the Aviary theme.

Double Bogie - 2 over Par on one hole. Nothing over this score counts towards a handicap. Triple is reduced to a double for handicap reporting purposes.

Handicap - Allows golfers of different skill levels to compete evenly. It is calculated by averaging your best 7 out of ten scores and subtracting that number from Par. ie. Avg 82 Par 72= 10 handicap.

> Scratch Player- a zero handicap. To play evenly against a 10 handicaper the Scratch player
> would give him 1 shot per hole on the 10 hardest holes

Stymie- An obstacle blocks the path of the ball to the hole.

Tunement- Augusta National Chairman Hootie Johnson's pronunciation of Tournament; good enough for me!

Toter - Any drink made to "tote" with you.

One for the Ditch - A drink made for the road. To "tote" with you when you leave. Generally used instead of "toter" when you don't need another. You generally have a very good chance of ending up in the ditch! I suspect this term has been around since horse drawn cart days.

Transfusion- A delightful concoction of Welches grape juice, Canada Dry ginger ale, and Voka. Famously served on the 10th Tee Box at Augusta National Golf Club. Virgin Transfusion- No Voka.

Norrised- When a playing partner exclaims "That's In" before the ball actually falls into the cup, causing the ball to miss the hole. Like BlackCatting. Named for Spring Valley Member Norris Watkins who famously invoked this "call" after anyone hit a putt. Late sixties, early seventies "He Norrised me"! I heard the term used by a stranger in California in the nineties. When I questioned him if he knew Norris, he said no, that everyone at his Club in Ohio used the term and no one knew where it had originated ?

Bingo Bango Bongo- Gambling game. Three points per hole. First person on the green-Bingo-1 point. Person closest to the hole-Bango-1 point. Longest putt made-Bongo-1 point.

Whiff- Swing at the ball and miss it completely.

Foot Wedge- Kick the ball.

Mouth wedge- Needling an opponent into making a bad shot.

Frozen Rope- A long straight shot normally low to the ground.

Worm Burner- A shot that never gets airborne.

Bass ball- Next shot to be played by a bass.

Luca Brasi- Sleeps with the fishes.

Linda Ronstadt- "Blue Bayou" Statement made as you walk by your opponents ball after outdriving them. My favorite song by Linda Ronstadt "Blew by You"!

Tips- As far back in length that a course can be played.

Bite- Calling for a ball to stop. Backspin put on a ball.

Break- The amount of curve in a ball running along the

ground, caused by slope, grain of grass, or wind.

Bunker- Sandtrap.

Casual water- Accumulation of water generally not found
in that spot. Not a hazard. Scoundrels have been known
to urinate on a ball and declare "casual water". Fisticuffs
generally are used to determine whether or not to grand a
drop.

Choke- Nerves effecting a players ability to perform.
Related terms include, "Take the Gas", "Collar got tight",
A gas truck pulled up. "Gagging". Can manifest itself
in a variety of physical ailments. Shaking, sleeplessness,
inability to tee up a ball, stuttering, stammering, difficulty
in swallowing, irritable bowels, inability to pull a club back
especially a putter, coordination is affected.

Cup- Hole. A 4.5"diameter circle cut into a green. A
plastic or metal insert is placed into the hole to hold
the flagstick or pin. A flag or in some places a basket(at
Merion) may be placed on top of the pin to show the player
the position of the hole.

Cut shot- A small slice or fade favored by better players for
control.

Draw shot- A small hook. Goes farther than a fade and
fights the wind better.

Divot- Any marring of the playing surface by a club hitting
a ball or a ball landing.

Dog Leg- Refers to a golf hole that bends. Not a straight
hole. Right or left.

Drop area- An area designed for a player to drop his ball
after taking a penalty for hitting into a penalty area, hazard.

Etiquette- Rules/ Suggestions as to how a golfer should behave while playing golf or being on the Club grounds.

Fore- A warning shouted to alert a person who may be in danger of being hit by a struck ball.

Gimmie- "In the Leather" "Throwback". Conceded that the player will sink the putt. Can only have a "gimmie" in competition if it is a matchplay format. There is no "gimmie" in medal play.

Grain- Direction the grass is growing. With the flow of water or towards the setting sun. The ball will roll easier with the direction of the grain than against it. Cross grain putts may curve in the direction the grass is growing. Different strains of grass have more or less grain. One of the finer points of golf, generally not concerning higher handicappers. (Alcohol) May be substituted for Voka in most recipes.

Greens fee- Cost to play a round of golf.

Greens in Regulation- Regulation to hit the ball onto a green is two shots less than par.

Greenie- Closest ball to the hole in a group. Must be on the green.

Grip- How you hold the club in your hands or the wrap that covers the shaft of the club. Many variations of both.

Gross score- refers to the number of strokes you may use to complete your round including penalty strokes. Subtracting your handicap will give you your "net"score.

Ground under repair- An area of the course undergoing repair and is unfit for play. Must be marked and a "drop zone " is generally provided.

Grounding- Placing the clubhead on the ground.

Halfway House- Generally located between the 9th and 10th holes for refreshments, snacks and restrooms(Voka at finer esablishments). More prevalent in Europe.

Handicap- A numerical representation of a golfer's playing ability if used properly. If not, a license to steal.

Hard pan- Bare ground. Skilled players prefer this to long grass as the ball can be controlled easier.

Home course- Course where a player establishes his handicap.

Honors- The right to Tee off first. Established by coin toss or lowest score on previous hole.

Hosel- Part of the clubhead that attaches the shaft. Hitting the ball here is called a "shank"!

Loft- The amount of angle on the face of the club. The higher the loft angle the higher and shorter the ball travels. Low loft 10* is for drivers and putters.

Mulligan- there are no mulligans in tournaments. A do over shot that doesn't count against the total score. Selling Mulligans is a big fundraiser for Charities that hold Golf Tournaments.

Nassau- A common gambling game that has three bets. One bet for the front and back nines and one bet for the eighteen hole round.

Nineteenth hole- Course's bar.

OB or Out of Bounds- Marked by white stakes designates the boundary of the course. Hitting the ball outside of these stakes results in a stroke and distance penalty.

Playing thru- Passing a slower group during the course of a round.

Provisional Ball- To speed the pace of play a player may play a second ball in case the first ball is thought to be lost or OB.

Rating- The measure of a courses difficulty.

Ready golf- Ignores the honor system that calls for players farthest away to play first, or had the lowest score on the previous hole.

Rough- Longer grass that borders the fairway. Second cut.

Shotgun start- Players are sent to separate holes around the course and start when a shotgun is fired.

Slope- Another measure of difficulty of the course.

Sit- =Bite

Smoked- A term for a long shot hit very well. Generally a drive.

Snake- A long putt holed.

Snowman- Making an 8 on a hole.

Sticks- Golf clubs

Stimpmeter- A devise used to measure the speed of a green. Resembles a skijump. Rolling a ball down this devise and measuring the distance it rolls gives a "Stimp" measure. 6'slow, 9'medium, Augusta National 13' quick!(mark a ball on greens this fast with a dime and the dime will slide)!

Sucker pin- A difficult pin position that suckers you into trying to hit the ball close to it.

Temporary Green- Often cut out of the fairway while the

regular green is under repair.

Tending the Flagstick- Until recently a player was assessed a stroke penalty for putting his ball into a flagstick if he were on the green. 2019 the rule was changed. Now a player may use the flagstick.

Trolley- Pullcart. Generally this term is used in Europe.

Waggle- Constant movement of the club at address in order to prevent a static address position.

Whiff- Missing the ball completely after a full swing intending to hit the ball.

Yips- The inability to move the club. Generally attributed to nerves. Older players exhibit this more than youngsters. Declining eyesight is a supposed cause. Ben Hogan famously could not pull the putter back. Smaller muscles are more subject to this condition.

Zone- Like a pitcher pitching a no hitter. Everything goes in the hole. Chevy Chase in "Caddy Shack", NANANanana was famously in the "zone". Backhanding balls into the hole, kicking balls into the hole....Can't miss!

Best Golf Courses
I've Played in South Carolina

Long Cove Club   Hilton Head Island

Yeamans Hall Hanahan

The Dunes Club   Myrtle Beach

Harbor Town Golf Links Hilton Head

Tidewater Golf Club North Myrtle Beach

Cherokee Plantation Yemmassee

Sage Valley Golf Club Graniteville

Musgrove Mill Golf Club Clinton

Camden Country Club Camden

Palmetto Golf Club Aiken

Ocean Course Kiawah Island

Secession Golf Club Beaufort

Cassique Kiawah Island

Columbia Country Club Columbia

Bulls Bay Bulls Bay

Charleston Country Club Charleston

Chanticleer Greenville

May River Golf Club Bluffton

Colleton River Bluffton

Debordeiu Debordeiu

Best Golf Courses
I've Played   United States

Augusta National Golf Club   Augusta, Georgia

Cypress Point   Pebble Beach, California

Pinehurst #2   Pinehurst, North Carolina

Pebble Beach Golf Links   Pebble Beach, California

Frederica Golf Club St. Simons Island, Georgia

San Francisco Golf Club San Francisco, California

East Lake Golf Club   Atlanta, Georgia

Olympic Golf Club   San Francisco, California

Bayonet Course, Fort Ord Monterrey, California

Inverness Golf Club   Toledo, Ohio

Merion Golf Club   Ardmore, Pennsylvania

Pinehurst #4   Pinehurst, North Carolina

Grandfather Mountain Golf Club Linville, NC

Quail Hollow Club Charlotte, North Carolina

Mid Pines Golf Club Southern Pines, NC

Congressional Golf Club   Washington, DC

Country Club of North Carolina Pinehurst, NC

Monterey Peninsula Country Club Monterrey, CA

Best Golf Courses
I've Played International

St. Andrews The Old Course St. Andrews, Scotland

Carnoustie Golf Links Links Parade, Scotland

Royal Portrush Portrush, Ireland

Portmarnoch Golf Links Portmarnoch, Ireland

Ballybunion Golf Club Ballybunion, Ireland

Cordoba Golf Club Cordoba, Argentina

Gullane Golf Club #1 Gullane, Scotland

Lahinch Golf Club Lahinch, Ireland

Prestwick Golf Club South Ayrshire, Scotland

Royal County Down Golf Club Newcastle, Ireland

Waterville Golf Links Waterville, Ireland

Old Head Golf Links Kinsale, Ireland